We believe that *Created* to those who have taken the Bible study, "Focusing on Christian Womanhood," and those who haven't. It is a thought-provoking, practical application of scriptural truths, and an uplifting way to begin your day.

—Alvena Blatchley, TRI-R Ministries

Created with Purpose is a heartfelt, wise, and honest devotional. Most of the Christian women I know want to know what God's will is for their lives. The world we live in makes that difficult to discern. Holly Eggert points us to the Lord God and the truth of His Word for the answers. I am confident her uplifting devotional will encourage your hearts and minds.

—Christine Whitehead, Preschool Teacher

CREATED *With* PURPOSE

A Daily Devotional Guide for Women

CREATED *With* PURPOSE

A Daily Devotional Guide for Women

HOLLY EGGERT

CREATED WITH PURPOSE by Holly Eggert
Published by Creation House
A Charisma Media Company
600 Rinehart Road
Lake Mary, Florida 32746
www.charismamedia.com

This book or parts thereof may not be reproduced in any form, stored in a retrieval system, or transmitted in any form by any means—electronic, mechanical, photocopy, recording, or otherwise—without prior written permission of the publisher, except as provided by United States of America copyright law.

Unless otherwise noted, all Scripture quotations are from the New King James Version of the Bible. Copyright © 1979, 1980, 1982 by Thomas Nelson, Inc., publishers. Used by permission.

All references are from *Focusing on Christian Womanhood* ©2007 TRI-R Ministries, Denver, Colorado.

Design Director: Bill Johnson
Cover design by Karen Gonsalves

Copyright © 2014 by TRI-R Ministries
All rights reserved.

Visit the author's website: www.hollyeggert.com

Library of Congress Cataloging-in-Publication Data: 2014902930
International Standard Book Number: 978-1-62136-740-6
E-book International Standard Book Number: 978-1-62136-741-3

While the author has made every effort to provide accurate telephone numbers and Internet addresses at the time of publication, neither the publisher nor the author assumes any responsibility for errors or for changes that occur after publication.

First edition

13 14 15 16 17 — 987654321
Printed in Canada

Dedicated to my husband, our children, and future generations of our family, in the name of Jesus and for the glory of God.

ACKNOWLEDGMENTS

*With acknowledgment and thankfulness
for her contribution to this book
Alvena Blatchley*

CONTENTS

Preface xiii
Introduction xv
Chapter 1: The Creation of Man and Woman 1
   A Change of Heart 2
   Created with Purpose 3
   Man First 4
   Man's Dominion 5
   Man's Moral Responsibility 6
   Man's Need for a Companion 7
   Man's Woman 8
   Leaving Home 9
   Working As One 10
   Marriage Is Very Good 11
   Do We Have To? 12
   The Tree of Knowledge of Good and Evil 13
   Falling for the Lie 14
   Hiding from the Truth 15
   Certain Judgment 16
   Certain Judgment, Part Two 17
Chapter 2: The Man's Role 19
   Exercising Dominion 20
   Final Decisions 21
   Subdue the Earth 22
   Multiply 23
   Tend the Territory 24
   Keep Watch 25
Chapter 3: The Woman's Role 27
   The Contented Woman 28
   Companion 29
   Helper 30
   Limited Dominion 31
   A Woman's Attitude 32
Chapter 4: When Things Go Wrong 33
   When Things Go Wrong 34

    Where Did We Go Wrong? 35
    Going the Extra Mile 36
    Self-Examination 37
    Further Self-Examination 38
    Steps to Forgiveness 39
Chapter 5: The Christian Woman and Her Children 41
    The Father Image 42
    The Mother Image 43
    A Child's Place 44
    A Parent's Example 45
    The Loving Parent 46
    The Mature Mother 47
    God's Capable Woman 48
    Mothers Teach Children about God 49
    A Mother's Son 50
    Mothers Are Not Perfect 51
    Mothers of Infants 52
    More Mothers of Infants 53
    Mothers of Children 54
    Mothers of Teens 55
    The Single Mother 56
    The Single Mother and Child Care 57
    Mother-In-Law 58
    Daughter-In-Law 59
    Married Daughters 60
    Grandmothers 61
    Grandmothers and Natural Grandchildren 62
    Grandmothers and Step-Grandchildren 63
    Grandmothers Bringing Up Grandchildren 64
Chapter 6: The Christian Woman and Home Management 65
    Home Management 66
    A Working Attitude 67
    Love Your Neighbor 68
    Competent Professionals 69

Teaching Younger Women	70
Hospitality	71
Chapter 7: The Christian Woman Herself	**73**
A Picture of Beauty	74
Inner Beauty	75
Inner Beauty and Dependence upon God	76
Inner Beauty and Peace with God	77
Inner Beauty and Inner Joy	78
Inner Beauty and Dependence on Husbands	79
Inner Beauty and Dependence on Others	80
Outer Beauty	81
Outer Beauty and Appearance	82
Outer Beauty and Countenance	83
Chapter 8: The Christian Woman, Her Church and Other Activities	**85**
Church and Activities	86
A Wife's Relationship to the Church	87
Submissive Conduct in Church	89
Silent Conduct in the Church	90
Teaching Other Women	91
Serving Others	93
Not Responsible	94
Priorities	95
When Employment Is Required	96
When Employment Is Not Required	98
Chapter 9: The Christian Woman, Her Growth and Maturity	**99**
Growth and Maturity	100
God Will Strengthen a Woman's Foundation	101
Postscript	103
Notes	105
About the Author	107
Contact the Author	109

PREFACE

And it happened, as He spoke these things, that a certain woman from the crowd raised her voice and said to Him, "Blessed is the womb that bore You, and the breasts which nursed You!" But He said, "More than that, blessed are those who hear the word of God and keep it!"
—Luke 11:27–28

WELCOME TO CREATED WITH PURPOSE, a daily devotional guide for women. The Lord Jesus Christ had a clear definition of being a blessed person: one is blessed who hears God's words, and carries them out. He knew that He would not have been born of Mary, nurtured by her, and given to the world to be our Savior, had she not first listened to and obeyed God's will and purpose for her life, which was announced by the angel Gabriel to her as a young virgin (Luke 1:26–38).

I wrote this book after studying and teaching the Bible study, *Focusing on Christian Womanhood*. As I studied, my confidence grew in God's design for me as a wife, mother, and homemaker, and I committed myself to pursuing excellence in these roles. With a clear sense of God's purpose guiding my life, I felt peace with myself, with others, and with God.

As I taught the Bible study to women, I noticed that my students were profoundly impacted by their discovery and application of these important truths. An unmarried college student was no longer ashamed of her femininity and her hope to someday be a godly wife and mother. A mother of teenagers found that her marriage had improved and her faith in God had grown deeper. A wife and mother of adult children was confronted with God's design for women for the first time, and made changes in her priorities and use of time.

You may be a Christian woman who is fighting the pull of a worldly culture and need encouragement to persevere in your faith. Maybe things have gone wrong, and you don't know how to make things right. My prayer is that these daily readings and reflections will lead you to God's high calling for you which He has revealed in the Holy Scriptures, and cause you to be confident, effective, and influential in your God-given roles and to enjoy being a Christian woman.

—Holly Eggert
Boulder, Colorado

INTRODUCTION

The story is told of a man who, as a child, had heard the story of the baby, Moses, "in the bulrushes" more times than he could count. In college, he majored in petroleum engineering, and with knowledge and experience as an oil industry executive, he re-read the account of Moses. As he read Exodus 2:3, which says that Moses's mother daubed the basket with pitch, it struck him that where there was pitch, there was oil. He conducted research to find the approximate site where the story of Moses took place. In doing so, he discovered a rich source of oil in the Middle East fields that have figured so prominently in modern history.

The Bible was not written as a scientific handbook, but if read carefully, the facts recorded in the Scriptures can give insights into areas not specifically addressed in the passage. Although the Bible was not written as a handbook on interpersonal relationships between men and women, a careful reading of the Genesis creation story can be the key to unscrambling many misunderstandings between men and women— or more specifically, between husbands and wives. When the story of the marriage relationship of Adam and Eve is read or told to children, seldom is the child looking for ways to understand the opposite sex in order to work with them or maintain any type of relationship with them. However, when this account is read from an adult perspective, there are points that draw attention to God's plan.

When God created any creature, He first had in mind the circumstances under which He wanted that creature to live and the functions He wanted it to perform. God created each creature with the physical and mental capability, as well as the drive or natural inclination, to do what He intended. God wanted birds to fly, so He gave them wings and the natural instinct to fly.

In the same way, prior to the creation of man, God had tasks in mind for mankind. He put into men and women not only the physical capacity, but also the *drive* to do these things, and He gave them a sense of satisfaction and pleasure as a reward for doing them well. Women who know and follow God's design for them will experience the same satisfaction and fulfillment as His reward.

CHAPTER 1

THE CREATION OF MAN AND WOMAN

The Creation of Man and Woman
A CHANGE OF HEART

"For My thoughts are not your thoughts, nor are your ways My ways," says the Lord.
—Isaiah 55:8

God can permanently change a woman's desires and drives.

Today there are countless self-improvement programs, counselors, seminars, and books that can assist a person with a problem area in his or her life. A few people, by sheer determination and strong character, can maintain a semblance of control over the behavior for a long period of time. Most are faced with defeat in a comparatively short time. In order to have permanent and complete improvement, there needs to be a change of basic desires and drives. God can make that change in the heart of a Christian woman.

In today's verse, the Bible teaches that human hearts are not naturally in tune with God's ideas; therefore, the type of change God desires cannot originate in a woman's mind nor be carried out by sheer human will. Often God's plan is not in tune with her self-improvement goals. The nature of a person leads her in the opposite direction from God's way. A woman may say, "I've got to get a hold of myself," and God says, "Let go, and I will work."

This daily devotional guide provides scriptures and explanations of the drives within men and women that lead them to do God's will. As a woman becomes more knowledgeable of these drives she can, with the Lord's help, put forth the effort to build a happier relationship with a man. Often a man responds by expressing interest in doing his part to enrich the relationship.

For Your Reflection

Do you believe that the Holy Scriptures are a guide for your life of faith and conduct? If so, are you open for God to change you to conform to His plan for you as a woman?

The Creation of Man and Woman
CREATED WITH PURPOSE

In the beginning God created the heavens and the earth.
—Genesis 1:1

God created all the Earth as the setting for man and woman.

In the first chapter of Genesis, God created the Earth, its atmosphere, and all plants and animals in sequence, and with order. As examples, God's order can be observed in the Earth and its atmosphere, in the creation of the atom, the solar system, the water system, the lunar tides, and the coral reefs. Plants and animals reflect His order in the creation of photosynthesis, pollination, the cellular system, metamorphosis, and the circulatory and skeletal systems.

God had an order, a design, and purpose for each of His creations, and functions for each to perform to do His will. He is the ultimate authority over all things: "The earth is the Lord's, and all its fullness, the world and those who dwell therein" (Ps. 24:1). God is the only One who truly understands what every creature was created to do and what circumstances each needs to perform at its highest level. God created all the Earth to be the setting for His highest creation, man and woman, made in His image.

For Your Reflection

How do you respond to God, knowing that He is your Creator? Do you believe that He knows you, knows what He created you to do, and knows what you need?

The Creation of Man and Woman
MAN FIRST

So God created man in His own image; in the image of God He created him; male and female He created them.
—GENESIS 1:27

God had a purpose in creating the man first.

GOD'S IMAGE IS noted in both male and female, but His first creation made in His image was the male. Human beings were His highest creation because they were created in His image.

Man did not evolve from animals. The Scriptures plainly teach that the creation of man from the dust of the earth was an act of God, separate from the creation of animals. God created man "in His own image" and God "breathed into [man's] nostrils the breath of life" (Gen. 2:7). Man, not animals, was also created with a spirit, making possible a relationship with God. This was certainly not the same for animals. In this day of New Age and Eastern philosophies, Christians must be careful to adhere to the authority of Scripture.

God created each creature with the physical and mental capability, as well as the drive or natural inclination, to do what He intended. Prior to the creation of man, God had five tasks in mind for him. According to Scripture, these five drives were: 1) to exercise dominion over the rest of God's creation; 2) to subdue the earth, which means to bring the forces of nature under his control; 3) to multiply, which is the sex drive, or the drive to reproduce; 4) to dress or tend the garden, his territory or place of special responsibility; and 5) to keep or protect what God had entrusted to him.

Note also that the man was formed first, not both sexes at the same time. The man was not created for the woman, but the woman was created for the man, who was formed first (1 Cor. 11:8–9).

∽

FOR YOUR REFLECTION

What is your response to the fact that God created man before woman?

The Creation of Man and Woman
MAN'S DOMINION

*Then the LORD God took the man and put him
in the garden of Eden to tend and keep it.*
—GENESIS 2:15

God created man first with specific purposes and work to do.

ALL CREATED THINGS on earth were to be under the authority of man. Instead of leaving Adam to exercise dominion over the entire world, an impossible task for one man, God gave him a smaller, specific territory, called the Garden of Eden, over which he was to have particular authority. God expressed two more purposes He had for man, namely to dress and to keep the garden. The word *dress* means to tend or to work in the garden, and *keep* refers to guarding, protecting, and taking care of the garden.

Is it surprising that work needed to be done in the Garden of Eden? When God created man, He created a body that thrives on work and physical exercise. Without these, a man's body would deteriorate and his muscles would atrophy. God also gave man a territory, a place where he lived and worked, and would someday have a family. It was man's responsibility to see that it was properly cared for and protected. In other words, the man was responsible for the protection of all that God had entrusted to him within his territory.

FOR YOUR REFLECTION

How is the drive to tend expressed in your father, husband, son, boyfriend, or boss? In what ways do they guard and protect you?

The Creation of Man and Woman
MAN'S MORAL RESPONSIBILITY

*And the L*ORD *God commanded the man, saying, "Of every tree of the garden you may freely eat; but of the tree of the knowledge of good and evil you shall not eat, for in the day that you eat of it you shall surely die."*
—**GENESIS 2:16–17**

Man is responsible for living within the boundaries set by God.

WHERE WAS EVE when this command was given? She hadn't been created yet as is evident in the words, "...God commanded the *man*..." The only moral law God gave was given to Adam, and it concerned the matter of obedience to God's word with regard to one tree. Here are seen both God's abundant generosity and man's moral responsibility to live within a large, but not unrestricted, circle of his God-ordained existence. For the man to step outside that circle to attempt to live an existence independent from God and His commands would be man's ruin. Because Adam was given the command, he became responsible for passing it on. He was also responsible for enforcing it.

FOR YOUR REFLECTION

By what actions or words has your father and/or husband conveyed his dependence on God? How has he seen that his family follows his example?

The Creation of Man and Woman
MAN'S NEED FOR A COMPANION

*And the LORD God said, "It is not good
that man should be alone."*
—GENESIS 2:18

A man was created to live in marriage relationship with a woman.

IN THE FIRST chapter of Genesis, after each of the first five days of His creation, God looked at what He had made and said, *"It is good."* In Genesis 2:18, however, God said that something was not good. His creation was incomplete. Adam, being made in God's image, had no other creature like himself with whom to have fellowship, and God said Adam needed someone for companionship.

What other needs did Adam have in this perfect environment? Man needed a helper. Woman was God's provision for man's needs for fellowship and help. Surprisingly, God did not immediately create this helper. Instead, He paraded the animals before Adam to name them (Gen. 2:19–20). By giving Adam this task, He gave him the opportunity to exercise authority over creation. While Adam was considering names for the animals, perhaps he noticed that there was no creature in the garden that shared his nature. He discovered his own unique superiority over all the animals, but God gave him the setting in which to feel his own solitude in the world.

FOR YOUR REFLECTION

What kind of companionship do you provide for your husband? How do you help your husband? How do the men you know seek companionship and help from women?

The Creation of Man and Woman
MAN'S WOMAN

And the Lord God caused a deep sleep to fall on Adam, and he slept; and He took one of his ribs, and closed up the flesh in its place. Then the rib, which the Lord God had taken from man He made into a woman, and He brought her to the man. And Adam said: "This is now bone of my bones and flesh of my flesh; she shall be called Woman, because she was taken out of Man."
—Genesis 2:21–23

The woman was created from the man's body.

Eve was not made entirely from the dust of the earth as Adam was; instead her source was man. She was "Adam's glory," as the Bible verse reads, "...but woman is the glory of man" (1 Cor. 11:7). She was created from him and for him. The name Adam gave her, *Woman*, indicates that he thought her most important characteristic was that she was taken out of him.

Because Eve was actually a part of Adam, all married couples since enjoy the same relationship. This explains the mystery of marriage—how two people from different backgrounds, each vowing in the presence of God to keep himself or herself only to each other, actually become "one flesh." Once they have been joined together by God, husband and wife are more akin to each other than to any other blood relative. Industry, business, and government recognize this "next of kin" relationship between husband and wife. It is expected of married women that the husband's name will occupy the space beside "closest living relative."

For Your Reflection

Do you see married couples that seem to be "one flesh"? If so, how do they behave? If married, how have you made yourself a part of your husband's life, body, and person? How do you "reflect" your husband's glory (1 Cor. 11:7)?

The Creation of Man and Woman
LEAVING HOME

Therefore a man shall leave his father and mother and be joined to his wife, and they shall become one flesh.
—**Genesis 2:24**

A man must have his own territory separate from his parents.

Problems arise when a husband (or wife) feels more closely related or more loyal to his (or her) father and mother than to his wife (or husband). God commanded the man to leave his father and mother because He expected each man to be responsible for his own territory.

As boys grow and mature into men, they develop a sense of territory. Sometimes their instinctive desire to have control over it infringes upon their father's territorial authority, causing conflict. This is a healthy situation because it encourages the son to prepare to leave home and to establish his own place to live.

When he grows up and marries, he is driven to be responsible for his own family. To do so, a son must take his wife to a new place, out from under the authority of his father, so that he can exercise dominion in a home of his own.

God emphasized the command for a man to leave his father and mother when Jesus repeated it to His disciples (Matt. 19:5). He knows what is best for His children, and wants to be obeyed and trusted for His love.

For Your Reflection

How has your father or husband established autonomy from his parents?

The Creation of Man and Woman
WORKING AS ONE

Then God blessed them, and God said to them, "Be fruitful and multiply; fill the earth and subdue it; have dominion over the fish of the sea, over the birds of the air, and over every living thing that moves on the earth."
—GENESIS 1:28

A husband and wife perform some God-given functions together.

BY GOD'S DESIGN, there are three functions men and women perform together: to multiply and fill the earth, to subdue the earth, and to have dominion over it. Since God's desire is to have a race of people who love Him in return for His kindness, He created man and woman with the physical capacity, as well as the instinctual desire, to propagate themselves. A man's sex drive, a woman's ability to conceive and her desire for a child are plain examples of expression of the drive to multiply. Each has been given the sex drive to bring pleasure to one another in the sex act within marriage.

It is also God's will for man and woman together to subdue the earth. Nature, if allowed to become unbalanced, has the ability to destroy mankind. For example, men and women labor to control the forces of nature by inventing and using disinfectants, medicines, and machinery. Before Eve was created, Adam was given dominion or authority over the earth. He was the one in charge to name the animals and received instruction concerning the fruit of the tree of knowledge of good and evil. Dominion was given first to Adam, and then Eve was created to help him exercise it.

FOR YOUR REFLECTION

In humility, assess your skills and abilities that can be used to perform these God-given functions together.

The Creation of Man and Woman
MARRIAGE IS VERY GOOD

*Then God saw everything that He had
made, and indeed it was very good.*
—GENESIS 1:31

Marriage is a relationship in which to work out God's will.

GOD'S ORIGINAL PLAN for marriage between a man and a woman continued throughout New Testament times. Whenever Jesus was asked about marriage, He always referred those asking questions back to Genesis 1 and 2. The apostle Paul based all of his teaching concerning marriage and the family on these passages as well. Even today, those who follow God's original design as a model for marriage will tell you that it still works as well as it did back then. Marriage is an efficient relationship in which to work out God's will.

Why is today's divorce rate so high? Why is there so much tension in many surviving marriages? Why do same-sex couples want to marry? Perhaps because, from Creation, Adam and Eve found what *they* decided would be a "better" way than God's way. God knew that if men and women followed His plans, everything would work out best. Adam was content with God's provision, especially with God's love gift, Eve. But Eve was deceived; she allowed Satan to persuade her that God's way was not true (1 Tim. 2:14). Adam and Eve were secure as long as they obeyed God, but they decided to step out of His will and do things their own way.

FOR YOUR REFLECTION

How have you found a "better way" to conduct your dating relationship or marriage?

For further study, see 1 Corinthians 11:8–9; Ephesians 5:31; 1 Timothy 2:13.

The Creation of Man and Woman
DO WE HAVE TO?

Now the serpent was more cunning than any beast of the field which the LORD God had made. And he said to the woman, "Has God indeed said, 'You shall not eat of every tree of the garden'?"
—GENESIS 3:1

Sin occurs when mankind rejects God's instructions.

SATAN, DISGUISED AS a serpent, must have been present in the garden when he heard God's instructions to Adam regarding his territory. He heard God say, "Of every tree of the garden you may freely eat; but of the tree of the knowledge of good and evil you shall not eat" (Gen. 2:16–17). After the creation of Eve, the serpent chose to speak to Eve and not to Adam. He changed God's instructions slightly to imply that God was placing a severe limitation on them. By framing these thoughts as questions to Eve, he forced her to think through such possibilities and draw her own conclusions.

Up until that moment, Eve knew what her husband had shared with her about the rules of the garden. She didn't know that there was a so-called problem with God's instructions, which the serpent implied. The problem was to doubt God's love and care for them, and to believe that they could do better for themselves if they were independent from God's way.

FOR YOUR REFLECTION

Perhaps the root of your problems has stemmed from ignorance or unbelief of God and His plan for womanhood. Take this time to confess this to God and ask Him to convince you in these areas.

The Creation of Man and Woman
THE TREE OF KNOWLEDGE OF GOOD AND EVIL

And the woman said to the serpent, "We may eat the fruit of the trees of the garden; but of the fruit of the tree that is in the midst of the garden, God has said, 'You shall not eat it, nor shall you touch it, lest you die.'"
—GENESIS 3:2–3

Adam and Eve rejected their God-given roles.

EVE QUOTED GOD almost correctly, but added "nor shall you touch it" to compound the severity of God's command. Eve now saw the perfect provision of the garden as a place to live as flawed. No longer were there plenty of delicious trees from which to eat, but in the center of the garden, a forbidden tree. She toned down God's threat of punishment from, "you shall surely die" (Gen. 2:17), to a milder, less absolute, "lest you die."

> Then the serpent said to the woman, "You will not surely die. For God knows that in the day you eat of it your eyes will be opened, and you will be like God, knowing good and evil."
> —GENESIS 3:4–5

Satan lied to Eve when he said that man would not die if he disobeyed God's orders, and he accused God of lying to them. He quickly followed to convince Eve that God had a motive other than love with His restriction. Perhaps Eve felt the aggravation of an injustice that did not exist. The serpent, having planted the lie in her mind, was silent and allowed Eve's new perception of reality to grow and take its own course.

FOR YOUR REFLECTION

Have you acted independently of your husband? What consequences have followed as a result in your marriage and family? How can you discern if the advice of another is God's will?
For further study, re-read Genesis chapter 3.

The Creation of Man and Woman
FALLING FOR THE LIE

So when the woman saw that the tree was good for food, that it was pleasant to the eyes, and a tree desirable to make one wise, she took of its fruit and ate. She also gave to her husband with her, and he ate.
—GENESIS 3:6

The human race fell into sin over the issue of sex role reversal.

ADAM WAS TO be the leader and assume responsibility for his family, yet he allowed the deception to progress without any intervention. He should have at this moment reminded Eve of God's Word and prevented her from eating. Instead, he said nothing, abandoned his post as leader and followed his wife, who led him by eating first, and then offering to him. The Bible does not say that he took some and ate it. Eve gave it to Adam. Both were wrong and together they pulled the human race down into sin and death. God fulfilled His promise that if they ate of the tree, they would surely die, both physically (up to this point death had never occurred) and spiritually. It is striking that the human race fell over the issue of sex-role reversal.

Eve's trouble, like a woman's today, started when she stopped obeying God and when she neglected to approach the one in charge in order to discuss alternatives and come to a decision together.

Satan had devised a plan that would cause God's creatures to obey him. At this point, the kingdom of the world, formerly ruled by God, fell into Satan's hands, not to be restored until the Lord Jesus Christ regains His reign at the end of time when, "The kingdoms of this world have become the kingdoms of our Lord and of his Christ, and He shall reign forever and ever" (Rev. 11:15). Until that time, there will be rewards for those who choose to obey God by living according to His commands, and consequences for those who choose to disobey God by living apart from them.

FOR YOUR REFLECTION

How frequently do you ask your father or husband for his opinion before you make important decisions?

The Creation of Man and Woman
HIDING FROM THE TRUTH

Then the eyes of both of them were opened, and they knew that they were naked; and they sewed fig leaves together and made themselves coverings. And they heard the sound of the LORD God walking in the garden in the cool of the day, and Adam and his wife hid themselves from the presence of the LORD God among the trees of the garden.
—GENESIS 3:7–8

Men and women make excuses for not following scriptural principles.

WHEN ADAM AND EVE disobeyed God, they hid from Him. God knew what had happened and knew exactly where Adam was because He had watched the whole scene, just as He sees all that goes on in every life today. In the verses that follow, God called to Adam and gave him several chances to confess his sin because He loved him and wanted to restore him to fellowship with Himself. Adam continued to divert attention away from the disobedience, and instead discussed the side effects. He blamed Eve for giving him the fruit and God for giving Eve to him.

Likewise, Eve explained that the serpent deceived her, although she did confess that she ate the fruit. Both refused to face the truth of their sin or take the opportunity to confess their sin and ask for His forgiveness. Instead, they both chose to hide from God and the truth.

In response, God cursed the serpent first, the primary source of the sin in the Garden of Eden. Then He disciplined Adam and Eve. Yet, mercifully and lovingly, even after their disobedience, He gave them a promise of hope in the prophecy of a Seed to come from the woman, namely, Christ (Gen. 3:15).

FOR YOUR REFLECTION

What actions or thoughts do you have that you think remain hidden from God? Consider talking openly to God about them. True healing and growth follow confession and the will to do better next time (1 Kings 8:39–40).

The Creation of Man and Woman
CERTAIN JUDGMENT

*So the L*ORD *God said to the serpent: "Because you have done this, you are cursed more than all cattle, and more than every beast of the field; on your belly you shall go, and you shall eat dust all the days of your life. And I will put enmity between you and the woman, and between your seed and her Seed; He shall bruise your head, and you shall bruise His heel."*
—G<small>ENESIS</small> 3:14–15

To the woman He said: "I will greatly multiply your sorrow and your conception; in pain you shall bring forth children; your desire shall be for your husband, and he shall rule over you."
—G<small>ENESIS</small> 3:16

God reprimanded Eve for leading Adam.

G<small>OD ADDRESSED EACH</small> sinning party, starting with Satan, who was the primary source. He promised to put deep-rooted hatred between Satan and the Seed of the woman, the Lord Jesus Christ. Jesus Christ alone saves Adam's descendants from the sin into which they had fallen.

God's judgment on Eve affected her physically, because pregnancy and the bearing of children would be accompanied by great hardship. Eve's conception of children was multiplied because any children born before the Fall would not have died, because there was no death. After sin came into the world, children often die, so Eve's ability to conceive had to be multiplied in order to continue the race as God had planned.

God then reminded her of the command that her husband would rule over her. When God created Eve, He created her to be a companion and a helper. Before the Fall, He had already established her submission to Adam as the follower, not the leader. God reiterated Eve's need and desire for Adam and her position of submission, because she had usurped his role of leader.

F<small>OR</small> Y<small>OUR</small> R<small>EFLECTION</small>

Have you taken the lead in a relationship with a father or husband? If you have, what were the results of your choice?

The Creation of Man and Woman
CERTAIN JUDGMENT, PART TWO

Then to Adam He said, "Because you have heeded the voice of your wife, and have eaten from the tree of which I commanded you, saying, 'You shall not eat of it'; Cursed is the ground for your sake; in toil you shall eat of it all the days of your life. Both thorns and thistles it shall bring forth for you, and you shall eat the herb of the field. In the sweat of your face you shall eat bread till you return to the ground, for out of it you were taken; for dust you are, and to dust you shall return."
—GENESIS 3:17–19

God reprimanded Adam for submitting to Eve.

GOD'S PRIMARY PURPOSE intended for man was to be the head of the family. Adam's first sin was that he shirked his responsibility to lead his only family member, his wife, Eve. Instead of leading her, he listened to her voice and heeded it, instead of heeding God's voice. Every husband who follows Adam's example of standing by while his wife leads the family (sometimes astray) is not asserting his God-given leadership role and will answer to God. The principles examined so far are restated in the New Testament and they still apply today.

Each man has the drive to have his own territory and to exercise dominion over it. Men and women today sometimes decide that a better philosophy of life can be adopted rather than what the Bible reveals is God's way of life. Feminist philosophy has convinced many to abandon the concept of God-given instincts and for both sexes to act, think, and pursue life as if there were no differences. Male leadership as presented in Scripture is strictly a matter of governmental arrangement. Each sex is equally precious to God, and the role each fulfills in carrying out God's will is equally important.

FOR YOUR REFLECTION

This week, look at television, magazine, and movie promotions that portray reversed sexual roles. How has this culture impacted your own view of life and your behavior with men? If you are married, how has it influenced your choices as a couple?

CHAPTER 2
THE MAN'S ROLE

The Man's Role
EXERCISING DOMINION

Then God said, "Let Us make man in Our image, according to Our likeness; let them have dominion."
—Genesis 1:26

It's natural for a man to lead, to be responsible, and competitive.

GOD CREATED MANKIND to exercise dominion over the earth; however, He first put all of His creation under the dominion of Adam before Eve was created. Adam worked with God to name the animals, and God recognized his authority by accepting each name. Eve was created afterwards as Adam's companion and helper, and together, man and woman exercised dominion over the earth.

The first characteristic of the drive to exercise dominion is a "sense of responsibility." A young man considering getting married has a strong sense that he is taking on a huge responsibility. He will have to provide for more than just himself. He recognizes that his wife and any future children will also have to live with any unfortunate decisions he makes.

Another characteristic is "competition for authority." Authority is a priority in men's employment. A man may dream of owning his own business, being supervisor of his group, and being promoted. He will often take an unpleasant job because of the opportunity for advancement. He will advance until he has all the authority he can comfortably handle. The desire for a defined territory, for respect in his leadership role, and for confidence in his ability to perform his role are expressed when a man has the lead in his home and family. After discussions with his wife, the husband has the final authority in many areas. He may choose the town, neighborhood, or house where the family will live. He may make the final decisions about how the children are trained and educated. He may decide how money and family time is spent so that he can work, rest, and enjoy leisure time along with the other family members.

FOR YOUR REFLECTION

What is your response to the authority of God? How could you show more respect for the God-given drive of authority in the men in your life this week?

The Man's Role
FINAL DECISIONS

For the husband is head of the wife, as also Christ is head of the church; and He is the Savior of the body.
—EPHESIANS 5:23

God appointed man the governmental position of leader of his family.

IN ORDER FOR any organization to run successfully, it has to have a president or chairman, someone who has the tie-breaking vote and the authority to make final decisions. Otherwise there can be endless discussion and debate, stalemating progress, and a hopeless inability to arrive at a final decision. It is impossible to make decisions that please everyone. Even when the family unit is comprised of only two people, if each has different ideas, progress can be hindered continually unless there is a chairman with the authority to make binding decisions. God, in His wisdom, has appointed the husband as the chairman of his family, so that families who follow scriptural principles can operate efficiently.

By choosing the husband to lead the family unit, God did not imply that men were more intelligent or more spiritual than women, that they always make wiser decisions than women, or even that they always want to do the right thing. God knew all about men when He made the decision to give the final authority to them. He was aware of man's nature and limitations when He restated His desire in this matter in the New Testament (Eph. 5:22–24).

God's decision was not a criticism of women's abilities, but a governmental arrangement of the family. A woman is free to discuss her own views on factors that influence family decisions, but the final decisions remain the responsibility of the husband.

FOR YOUR REFLECTION

God has appointed this man to be your father or husband, regardless of his prior success or ability. How can you encourage him?

Suggestion for Prayer: Ask God to give you increased faith in His appointment of man as family leader.

The Man's Role
SUBDUE THE EARTH

Then God blessed them, and God said to them, "Be fruitful and multiply; fill the earth and subdue it."
—GENESIS 1:28

It's natural for a man to accept challenges in the face of adversity.

EACH OF THE natural instincts and drives of man were given for the purpose of bringing glory to God and expediting His purposes on earth. The drive to subdue the earth by bringing the forces of nature under control propelled a man to accept big challenges and kept him going in the face of adversity.

Some of the uncontrolled forces of nature could destroy life on earth. If men had not discovered herbs and invented medicines, people would have died prematurely from incurable diseases. Floods, avalanches, tornadoes, and hurricanes pose deadly threats to people, but men built dams, diverted water to good uses, blasted away avalanches, and designed warning systems for hurricanes and tornados so that people could take shelter. In order to encourage this drive, God gave men inventive minds, the desire to accept challenges, and inner satisfaction from invention and discovery.

The drive to subdue was given to women also, but this will not cause conflict in the husband/wife relationship if it is expressed according to the purposes for which God created woman. For example, a woman can sit up all night with a sick child, fighting the forces of nature which could take the child from them, or she can serve well-balanced, nutritious meals, and keep the home clean to help her family ward off disease.

FOR YOUR REFLECTION

Look for motivation and a go-getter attitude in the men you know. Show appreciation for his effort to meet a challenge.

Suggestion for Prayer: Pray that your husband, father, and sons will allow God to channel this drive into constructive use.

The Man's Role
MULTIPLY

*Then God blessed them, and God said to
them, "Be fruitful and multiply."*
—GENESIS 1:28

*A husband and wife exercise their sexual
drives freely with each other.*

GOD PLACED THE drive for sexual expression in the first man and woman. Sexual intercourse shared within the marriage relationship results in mutual joy and when it is God's will, the procreation of children. These children are gifts from God and He wants them to be nurtured in the knowledge and love of Him.

God created nothing that is in itself sinful. It is how the sex drive is used that determines its rightness. A healthy man exercises his drive freely with his wife and both receive the benefit of God's blessings. God states that a husband's and wife's bodies belong to each other (1 Cor. 7:2–9) for mutual joy, for continual satisfaction (Prov. 5:18–19), and for the expression of love and comfort in difficult times (Gen. 24:67).

In this day and age, it is hard to stay pure. However, abstaining from sexual activity is what God intended for unmarried persons. When people have sinned sexually, they can be fully restored by God by confessing the sin, then asking for His forgiveness and for His strength to resist temptation in the future.

∼

FOR YOUR REFLECTION

If you are single, how can you respond to the temptation to engage in sexual behavior? If married, do you have difficulty making the time, having desire and/or energy for a healthy sexual relationship with your husband?

The Man's Role
TEND THE TERRITORY

*Then the Lord God took the man and put him
in the garden of Eden to tend and keep it.*
—Genesis 2:15

A man works to make his home his haven.

WHAT WAS THE Garden of Eden to Adam? It was the source of his employment, but it was also his home where he would one day live with his wife and children. God gave man a particular territory and placed him as "head." A man's territory is the place where he lives and works. However, a man will consider his home his territory where his care and work give him a feeling of personal satisfaction. He will feel responsible for the upkeep of the house and grounds, painting, maintaining, and repairing the items in the home and the property around it. Men have more muscle mass, and straight back, arm, and leg construction that enable them to do heavy tasks without injury.

There are many decisions made when setting up a home. Many discussions are necessary to assure both husband and wife that they feel comfortable in their home. When a man takes part in decorating, choosing colors and furniture, plants and landscaping, he will feel at home anywhere in the house. When a man feels at home, he will enjoy tending his territory.

For Your Reflection

In what ways do you recognize the sense of territory in your husband, sons, father, brothers, or male co-workers? How can you show respect for this drive in them?

Suggestion for Prayer: Pray for God to guard your tongue from nagging and criticizing your husband as he makes your home a reflection of both his tastes and yours, and suitable to the needs and desires of both of you.

The Man's Role
KEEP WATCH

*Then the L*ORD *God took the man and put him
in the garden of Eden to tend it and keep it.*
—GENESIS 2:15

God appointed the man to protect what He entrusted to him.

THROUGHOUT HISTORY MEN have kept watch and protected others. In the Middle Ages, a knight swore to honor the laws of chivalry and fight to the death to protect his maiden. When the *Titanic* ship sank, men shepherded the women and children to safety, risking and losing their own lives. Men in the armed forces are willing to protect the safety of their country by self-sacrifice. On the home front, a man installs fences, door locks, and security alarms to protect his family from harm and his possessions from theft. He purchases life insurance, sets up trusts, and writes a will to protect his family from loss of income should he perish. When he travels alone away from home, he may also have a list of special instructions for his family to follow to ensure their safety.

A man provides spiritual protection and leadership for his family. Wives are advised to seek this protection (1 Cor. 14:35). When a wife asks her husband for help about spiritual matters, he will want to have the right answer and may seek help from a minister, the Bible, and/or prayer. His children will learn from her example to seek their father for their spiritual questions. In this way, he will provide spiritual leadership and protection for his family.

A man has the drive to make the final decisions, to subdue nature, to seek sexual release, to keep his home, and to protect his family. A wife may find them as stifling and controlling unless she understands God's design for men. Then, she can encourage and support his behavior and give him the satisfaction of full expression of these drives.

∽

FOR YOUR REFLECTION

Are you independent of your husband, father, or brother? If so, what have been the results of stepping out from under their protection?

CHAPTER 3

THE WOMAN'S ROLE

The Woman's Role
THE CONTENTED WOMAN

*Give her of the fruit of her hands, and let
her own works praise her in the gates.*
—Proverbs 31:31

A woman's mission will be fulfilled through her God-given roles.

The past daily readings have centered on men and women and the purposes for which God created them. The emphasis has been on the drives God instilled in them to help them fulfill God's purposes. Today's focus is on the woman and her God-assigned role.

There is great restlessness and discontent among women today. This may be from the lack of a clearly defined purpose in life. A woman feels her worth and sees progress in her life when she has well-defined goals and is able to see continual advancement toward their accomplishment. Lifelong goals remain constant through the stages of life, and when each stage has passed, there is still vision and energy to go on to the next stage and goal. How does a woman establish lifelong goals?

The Scriptures record that God had five jobs or functions for the woman to do when He created her. She was to be a companion, to be a helper, to be a mother, to exercise dominion, and to subdue the earth. The woman who concentrates on carrying out these purposes in her life and seeks to excel in each drive will be content. Lack of fulfillment, restlessness, and despair are the results when a woman's efforts are misdirected, and all her drives are not finding expression within God's purposes for her life.

For Your Reflection

You may be going off to college, a college graduate, working and raising children, a single mother, in the middle of life with an empty nest, alone without a husband, and/or elderly. Have you lost sight of your purposes? How could your God-given drives find expression in your circumstances today?

The Woman's Role
COMPANION

And the Lord God said, "It is not good that man should be alone."
—Genesis 2:18

God has given the woman a strong need to be a companion.

God decided in the beginning that a man needed a woman to keep him company. A companion is someone with whom you enjoy being, enjoy talking, enjoy discussing things, and enjoy going places. Most women have a strong desire for companionship, and since they were created to be companions, it meets a need in their lives. It is not emotionally or spiritually healthy for unmarried women and widows to isolate themselves from the companionship of others because of busyness or self-pity.

In order to meet this need for a man and to fulfill her own desire for companionship, one of a woman's lifelong goals is to learn how to be a good companion. There is no need for talk when she enjoys just being with and going places with a man. She can look for opportunities to accompany him, when it is suitable to him and his schedule. She can ask him if he would like her to go with him to run an errand, play a sport, have a meal together, or just sit beside him. Putting effort into looking and sounding pleasant enhances her attractiveness as a companion.

If a woman can learn the art of active listening, her husband, father, or boss will be very appreciative. Listening involves turning away from distractions, looking at him, and focusing on what he is saying.

Discussion of important matters is another skill needed to be a good companion. In a discussion, both of the parties have knowledge of the subject being discussed, they both have feelings on the matter, but neither has made up his mind previous to the discussion. If either has made up his mind, it generally ends in an argument.

For Your Reflection

Are you willing to learn to be a good companion to your husband? Having an attractive manner and appearance, being a good listener and conversationalist, and appreciating the value of companionship have lifelong benefits for you to enjoy.

The Woman's Role
HELPER

For man is not from woman, but woman from man. Nor was man created for the woman, but woman for the man.
—1 Corinthians 11:8–9

The challenge of being a helpmate will help a woman to mature.

WOMAN WAS CREATED for man, to meet his physical, psychological, emotional, and social needs. One of the ways she meets his physical needs is by creating a home for him. Homemaking is a career of great worth to God. Skills in housecleaning, planning, preparing and serving nutritious meals, and doing laundry and mending will help to provide a well-ordered haven where he resides. A wife can meet his physical needs as a sexual partner. A healthy sex life has lifelong benefits for husband and wife as it relieves tension, affirms closeness, and restores and reaffirms the marriage bond.

A wife can be a psychological helpmate to her husband to sustain his self-confidence, to maintain his self-respect, to have faith in his ideals, and to gain encouragement in reaching his goals. She can alleviate the emotional stresses he faces by being trustworthy in handling her responsibilities sensibly. He trusts her to care for the children properly, do the shopping, and spend money conservatively and wisely.

What is involved in being a helpmate in the social part of a marriage? A wife can meet and entertain members of her husband's family, his colleagues, his acquaintances made in the community, and his friends, in such a way that she is a complement to him. Together, they are a hospitable team, and her work in this area enhances his position in the community.

Being a helpmate physically, mentally, emotionally, and socially challenges a woman to mature. Achieving these lifelong goals is a matter of study and prayer, and working toward excellence. Since it is God who instructs a woman to be a good helpmate in all these areas, He will provide the strength.

For Your Reflection

Think of ways you can be helpful in his job, in social situations, or at home, without stepping into his role.

The Woman's Role
LIMITED DOMINION

Then God said, "Let Us make man in Our image, according to Our likeness; let them have dominion over the fish of the sea, over the birds of the air, and over the cattle, over all the earth and over every creeping thing that creeps on the earth."
—Genesis 1:26

A woman can exercise dominion within the boundaries of her role.

GOD FOUND IT necessary to give the drive to exercise dominion to both male and female in order to have His will accomplished. When her husband leaves the house, this drive motivates a wife to do her work at home.

Eve had the drive to exercise dominion, but she ran into a problem. There was a limit to her freedom in exercising dominion. Just as God held Adam responsible for what happened in the Garden of Eden, God made the husband ultimately responsible to Him for headship in the family. While the couple is "one flesh" and operate as a team, there will be times when the husband has to make the final choice. A wife's drive to exercise dominion is subject to his final approval.

As long as a wife exercises dominion within her role (for instance, by tending her home and children), and maintains a good attitude about it, her husband will not feel threatened, and can trust her to use creativity and the full expression of her gifts to fulfill this role.

For Your Reflection

How motivated are you to attend to your responsibilities? What goals have you set for yourself in these areas? Do you have supportive friendships and good role models available to you to help you? How can you make achieving your goals fun and rewarding?

The Woman's Role
A WOMAN'S ATTITUDE

Therefore, just as the Church is subject to Christ, so let the wives be to their own husbands in everything.
—Ephesians 5:24

A wife's submission to her husband reflects her submission to Christ.

A WOMAN'S DRIVES, WHEN expressed with the proper attitude, bring her a true sense of satisfaction. A woman can keep her house resentfully, or she can keep it out of respect for herself and love for her husband and children. With one attitude, she is a slave to the house, and with the other attitude, the house serves her. Since a woman's attitude is as important as the activities that make up her life, God was very explicit in His teaching as to what the Christian woman's attitude was to be, and that is an attitude of submission.

A submissive attitude is a heartfelt belief that God's greatest good for a woman lies in accepting and living the whole feminine role (companion, helper, mother) with a complete absence of desire to exercise authority over her husband or to usurp the role that God gave him. Belief in God and His Son, Jesus Christ, is the motivation to follow scriptural submission. Christ submitted to the Father when He suffered death on the cross for mankind. The Church submits to His leadership. A husband submits to Christ and a wife submits to her husband.

Each woman has to come to the place where she voluntarily surrenders herself to her husband as an act of obedience to God. Following this comes a heartfelt satisfaction with this kind of life, and results in a waning of the desire to usurp the man's God-given role.

～

For Your Reflection

Do you know a woman who submits to her husband? How would you describe her actions and her attitude? What is her husband's response to her?

CHAPTER 4
WHEN THINGS GO WRONG

WHEN THINGS GO WRONG

> *Pursue peace with all people...lest any root of bitterness springing up cause trouble, and by this many become defiled.*
> —HEBREWS 12:14–15

Marital trouble occurs when the degree of closeness declines.

IF A WOMAN has been reflecting, praying, and applying the truths of this devotional, God has changed more in her than she may realize. As she draws closer to Him, she may become aware of conflicts within herself and in her marriage that indicate that things have gone wrong. Since everyone has a different definition about what constitutes things going wrong, a few examples are needed to define the phrase.

A wife may comment that she and her husband never fight, but although there is no actual fighting, underneath the surface there are resentments, grudges, and obvious anger. The most lethal kind of fight a couple can have is where there is a disagreement, but all the anger is held inside.

Another wife may contend that she and her husband enjoy fighting. Fighting sets a poor example for their children because they may conclude that fighting is the only way to settle an argument. Secondly, when one partner likes to fight, the other may play along while he/she may not like to fight. For one person, all is forgiven and forgotten within minutes after a fight, but for the other, forgiveness may be difficult. Unresolved anger and unforgiveness, like seeds, can grow into bitterness in a person's heart.

Some couples avoid conflict by making little time to be together and going their own separate ways. When two lives that at one time were pledged to walk together begin to walk in different directions, the distance between them widens to the point where they realize they no longer need each other. Very often separation, divorce, or an extramarital affair is the result.

A definition of when things have gone wrong is *whenever the degree of closeness, love, and companionship you have attained in your relationship with your husband begins to decline, even slightly, things have gone wrong.*

FOR YOUR REFLECTION

In what areas have things gone wrong in your marriage?

When Things Go Wrong
WHERE DID WE GO WRONG?

Search me, O God, and know my heart; try me, and know my anxieties; and see if there is any wicked way in me, and lead me in the way everlasting.
—PSALM 139: 23–24

A wife can identify where things have gone wrong.

As a wife grows spiritually, she changes personally. Any change in her attitude or routine automatically calls for an adjustment on the part of her husband and family, and this can cause conflict. For example, if she believes that submitting to God's will for her requires submitting to her husband, she may find that as she practices this it is hard for him to step in and take over. Even though he knows he should take more responsibility, it will take extra time and energy for both of them to adjust.

Stress can be a cause of conflict for a wife when she discovers that her daily routine is affected by being physically tired, ill, or from the effects of her menstrual cycle. These pressures mount if she gets behind in her housework and tries to handle working outside the home, volunteering, childcare, or even planning a wedding. All of these stresses can strain her relationship with her husband.

A husband may feel pressure from his job, physical health problems, the responsibility of upkeep of the house and property, his children's problems, his aging parents' care, and financial difficulties. Sometimes a wife adds to his pressures by making complimentary comments about other men, implying that he is lacking in some way.

A woman must step back from her life and survey all the areas of it in order to identify where things seem out of sync. In order for her to do this effectively, it will be helpful for her to learn the practice of self-examination.

FOR YOUR REFLECTION

In what areas of your life are there conflicts? Are they in your marriage? Within yourself? Other areas?

When Things Go Wrong
GOING THE EXTRA MILE

And whoever compels you to go one mile, go with him two.
—Matthew 5:41

A wife was created to submit and adapt to her husband.

A WOMAN IS CALLED to *give* and *give some more* in order to make her husband feel like the most important person in her life. For one woman, this comes easily and seems to be part of her nature and personality. For another, it is the most difficult thing she has ever been called to do.

Sometimes when disagreements have come between wife and husband, it is because they are caught up in a vicious cycle of "returning evil for evil" (1 Pet. 3:9). A woman should break the pattern for two reasons. First, she was created to be the one to submit to her husband and adapt to the marriage relationship. Second, because of man's nature, the husband may find it difficult to admit defeat or to apologize.

There are many rewards for the woman who, with God's help, expresses the quality of humility and willingness to let go of her desires. Often, this will bring out gentleness in her husband, an unexpected gift, an apology, or a new spiritual quality in him. In this, as in many other areas, there is a mystery involved. Christ said, "If anyone desires to be first, he shall be last of all and servant of all" (Mark 9:35). God's economy works differently than man's economy. People believe that in order to have, one should save and keep. God says, "Give, and it will be given to you" (Luke 6:38).

∽

For Your Reflection

When do you find it hard to "go the extra mile" with your husband? Why do you resist? When you do let go of your own desires and make the extra effort, what is the result?

When Things Go Wrong
SELF-EXAMINATION

And why do you look at the speck in your brother's eye, but do not consider the plank in your own eye? Or how can you say to your brother, "Let me remove the speck from your eye"; and look, a plank is in your own eye?
—MATTHEW 7:3–4

Examining oneself first is a step to take when problems arise.

MANY TIMES WHEN a problem arises, a woman has not analyzed it and/or the situation, and feels helpless as to how to resolve it. The problem she faces may be the result of something she is doing that is keeping her out of fellowship with God and others, which she will discover by examining herself.

Let her consider her health. How is she feeling? When was her last physical examination by a licensed doctor? Is her menstrual cycle or hormonal balance affecting her? She can consider the present circumstances in which she lives: she may be behind in her work, caring for sick children, or entertaining houseguests, which cause fatigue. She may be facing financial or business problems that cause her to worry. She may be out of fellowship with God by neglecting to read the Bible or pray, or choosing to worry instead of prayer. Sometimes a woman starts a new spiritual discipline as a promise to God, such as weekly church attendance or daily prayer, and then abandons it. She may be angry with God for allowing her to suffer in her current unhappy circumstances, whatever they may be.

How about a despondent thought pattern? She may be feeling sorry for herself and holding a grudge against real or imagined slights from others. Often a grudge is the result of anger toward certain people or circumstances that turns into resentment, bitterness, and unforgiveness. If she is holding a grudge, it will do more harm to her than to the person toward whom she holds the grudge.

Once a woman has examined herself and discovered things that may be causing her unrest, she can examine her relationships with other people in her life.

FOR YOUR REFLECTION

Read through the Ten Commandments (Deut. 5:6–21) to examine your thoughts, words, and actions in light of them.

When Things Go Wrong
FURTHER SELF-EXAMINATION

First be reconciled to your brother.
—M<small>ATTHEW</small> 5:24

Examining relationships with others may reveal stress points.

A WIFE'S RELATIONSHIP TO her husband should take priority over others, with the exception of her relationship to God. Whenever the degree of closeness to her husband has declined, even slightly, a wife may discover why this has occurred by *examining her own behavior and attitudes.* Has she been stepping into his role? In what areas has she neglected his self-esteem? Which of his physical, emotional, and psychological needs has she neglected? What pressures does he have for which she is not making allowances? Overall, what is keeping her from being the companion and helpmate that she could be to him?

What about her relationship as a mother to her young or adult children? Has she neglected them in any way? Has she been unkind or impatient with them? What problems are unresolved with relatives? Has she been a good neighbor, and if so, how? Are there unresolved problems with people in the church? Has she been irritable with clerks or businesspeople?

An examination of these relationships will be helpful, but it doesn't imply that all the disagreements and disappointments are entirely her fault. If she finds that she has done something overtly wrong or is neglecting to do something that she should be doing, she can take steps toward reconciliation. She can thank the Lord for the lesson He will teach her through her present situation and then confess any known sin to Him. If she needs to make an apology, it should never be flippant or insincere, but she can make it a pleasant experience. Many men dislike tense, repentant scenes, so she can consider sending him a card, writing him a note, making his favorite dinner, or buying him a gift. A simple apology at an opportune time can be effective.

If a woman discovers that she is having difficulty forgiving someone who has asked for her forgiveness, she can consider the steps to forgiveness outlined above and on the next page.

F<small>OR</small> Y<small>OUR</small> R<small>EFLECTION</small>

How will you face your faults and change direction?

When Things Go Wrong
STEPS TO FORGIVENESS

And He said to me, "My grace is sufficient for you, for My strength is made perfect in weakness."
—2 Corinthians 12:9

Self-examination, repentance, and confession will lead to forgiveness.

WHEN SOMEONE HAS offended another person, hurt feelings result and a breach forms in the relationship. Sometimes the offender recognizes the offense and asks the offended person for forgiveness. When this occurs, the offended person has an opportunity to forgive the offender, and if he or she does forgive, the relationship is reconciled. The decision to forgive becomes the clearer choice when a woman has experienced being forgiven by God for her offenses. Once she has examined herself, become aware of her own sins, repented of them, and confessed them to Him to receive His forgiveness, the breach in her relationship with Him has been reconciled. To forgive is to decide before God that, with His grace, she will not allow herself to make the offender pay, even in small ways, for the offense done to her.

Once the decision has been made to forgive, it will take time for the wound to heal and action to bring about a successful outcome. If she waits until she feels like doing good things for her offender, she may never obey God. Forgiveness is sometimes hard from start to finish because it goes against all the tendencies of carnal nature. Jesus taught in a parable that the offender will need to be forgiven "seventy times seven" (Matt. 18:22), or over and over again, as the offense is recalled mentally and relived emotionally. However, it is possible for a woman to control her thoughts by forgiving repeatedly and choosing to forget the offense.

Forgiving actions she can take may include helping the offender when he or she is in trouble, rather than rejoicing and wishing hardship. She can ask God to bless him or her in her prayers. She can guard against gossip and slander of the offender. For God is always kind to unthankful and evil people and asks us to be merciful as He is.

~

For Your Reflection

What does God want to teach you through this offense? God corrects and disciplines His children for greater growth.

CHAPTER 5
THE CHRISTIAN WOMAN AND HER CHILDREN

The Christian Woman and Her Children
THE FATHER IMAGE

As Sarah obeyed Abraham, calling him lord.
—1 Peter 3:6

*A wife's respect for her husband teaches
her children to respect authority.*

THE FIRST STEP in godly parenting of children is for children to know what their relationship to their parents should be. Parents are responsible before God for their training and admonition from infancy through young adulthood. According to several passages in the Bible, the top of the line of authority is the father. Joshua spoke for his family when he said, "But as for me and my house, we will serve the Lord" (Josh. 24:15). Qualifications for bishops are defined as "one who rules his own house well, having his children in submission" (1 Tim. 3:4–5). God holds the husband and father responsible for the whole family over which he leads.

A mother's respect for the father creates in their children a respect for authority. By supporting his decisions, his discipline, and his instructions regarding the children, a man becomes confident in his role and the children learn that he *is* the final authority in their home. An unmarried mother can look to her father or a mature brother to establish this relationship with her children. If she has remarried, the stepfather has his place in the child's life and will need to have the mother's support in building a strong father image for the stepchild.

God loves and accepts each of His children. He watches over them, protects and provides for them, listens to, and answers them. He leads them, gives directions to them with built-in consequences for disobedience, yet He shows mercy to them when they sin. He is just, and there is safety in Him. These are the qualities a man needs to have to be a strong father image in his home. A wife and mother can assist her husband by praying for him, encouraging him, and respecting him, as God builds these qualities into his life.

For Your Reflection

What fatherly attributes have you observed in your husband? In what ways have you interfered with his authority? How do you speak of him to the children?

The Christian Woman and Her Children
THE MOTHER IMAGE

She opens her mouth with wisdom, and on her tongue is the way of kindness. She watches over the ways of her household, and does not eat the bread of idleness. Her children rise up and call her blessed; her husband also, and he praises her: "Many daughters have done well, but you excel them all."
—PROVERBS 31:26–29

A mother's love and time invested in her children pay rich dividends.

MOTHERHOOD IS FIRST mentioned in Genesis 1:28 when God commanded Adam and Eve to be fruitful and multiply. His plan was to propagate mankind who He created in His image. Children need nurturing and are unable to survive independently of others. A woman's drive to mother is expressed by the desire to have a child, satisfaction in caring for children, emotional involvement with the concerns of children, the desire to protect them, and a willingness to see her authoritative role as temporary.

In the past, the role of mother has been a very revered one. Many well-known people have pointed to a godly mother as the one who influenced them the most, thus the saying, "The hand that rocks the cradle rules the world." A woman's children observe the life of their mother lived before them to form an attitude toward women and motherhood.

In God's line of authority for the home, the mother is second-in-command and the one in charge when her husband is absent. When the father is away from the home, the mother is to be in control of the children and they are to obey her. When a woman understands this relationship, she can parent consistently and with assurance. She will be able to discard unsound advice offered by relatives, friends, teachers, doctors, books, and television shows.

The Christian mother desires that her influence on her children will lead them to respect motherhood and the laws of God, and to obey God's will for their lives.

FOR YOUR REFLECTION

To whom or to what do you look for guidance in your role as a mother? What people have most influenced you as a mother? What examples did they leave you?

The Christian Woman and Her Children
A CHILD'S PLACE

*Train up a child in the way he should go, and
when he is old he will not depart from it.*
—Proverbs 22:6

Children are entrusted to parents to be nurtured in love.

The Bible states that children are last in the line of authority in the family. God knew how long it would take to develop the ability to make wise decisions, so He put children under the authority of parents until they could do so. God holds the parents responsible for the children's welfare and each parent is obligated to make thousands of decisions for the child in his first few years.

If a child grows up without guidance and leadership, there are some things that are necessary for his proper maturation that he will never purposely choose for himself. One is learning to obey and take punishment constructively. God's way of teaching His children to obey Him is by having them learn as children to obey their parents. Next, other people with authority, like teachers and police, come into the child's life to further his education in obedience. If a child never learns to obey his parents and the law officers he can see, how can a parent expect him to accept direction and discipline from God, whom he cannot see?

Parents should consider making the basic rules that would always be true and apply them at home. When a child is very young, he needs many behavioral limits. As he grows older, he must be allowed a wider world. Children push outward in behavior until they meet a barrier. Parents should discuss and set limits, enforcing them within the family so that the child does not have to face punishment from relatives, friends, neighbors, school, or the law.

A parent's goal in disciplining his or her child in love is to have a mature individual who operates independently of the parents within his/her sex role.

For Your Reflection

Read the following Holy Scriptures about discipline from Proverbs 19:18; 29:17.

The Christian Woman and Her Children
A PARENT'S EXAMPLE

*And the L*ORD *visited Hannah, so that she conceived and bore three sons and two daughters. Meanwhile the child Samuel grew before the L*ORD.
—1 SAMUEL 2:21

Parents can teach their children to be comfortable in their sex roles.

A MOTHER SETS AN example for her daughter in the way she dresses, and in the attitudes she has about being female, in accepting her husband's authority, in doing her tasks around the home, and about other women. Being feminine in her heart will carry over into how she looks, how she thinks, how she talks, and how she walks. Daughters go through phases when they want to dress, talk, and walk like their peers, but overall, a mother's example will have an enduring impact on their lives.

In the same way, a father's attitude toward being male will be reflected in his appearance, speech, and countenance. His behavior toward his wife and his example of how to relate to a woman will influence his son's identity as a man and his future choices.

A mother's attitude toward her marriage is taught by example. A mother who is committed to and enjoys her role (obeys her husband, respects him, remains loyal to him, and serves him unselfishly) may be rewarded with a daughter who does the same for her husband, and a son who learns to provide for and protect his wife.

Children learn by their parent's example how to complement and compliment the opposite sex. They may recall that their parents found that there was a worthy purpose, sincere love, and security in living within the sex roles God assigned, and find it natural to adopt them in their own homes when they marry.

∽

FOR YOUR REFLECTION

What is your attitude toward being a woman? What kind of example have you set for your children?

The Christian Woman and Her Children
THE LOVING PARENT

And you, fathers, do not provoke your children to wrath, but bring them up in the training and admonition of the Lord.
—EPHESIANS 6:4

Parents can love their children with God's never-failing love.

THE PURPOSE OF discipline in the home is to encourage a child's obedience to authorities. God instructs His children with the Holy Scriptures; He allows His children to learn obedience to their own parents, teachers, or law enforcement officers. God gives commands with consequences for disobedience. God is both just and has a sense of humor. God sees all, knows all, and still loves His children too much to let each child remain as he/she is right now.

Love makes a difference in a parent's discipline techniques. A boy who is sent to bed early as a discipline by a loving father and later, kisses his father goodnight is in contrast to a boy who is disciplined by an unloving father in the same manner and becomes sullen, resentful, and rebellious.

Children sense a lack of love and acceptance when parents give them material things instead of their love and time. No child is spoiled by love. A child is spoiled by indulgence. Children will need correction for disobeying a clearly stated rule of the parents. When a child is corrected, parents can offer constructive suggestions of how the child can attain the desired behavior with an attitude of acceptance, love, and help.

FOR YOUR REFLECTION

Have you lovingly set limits for your children? What is your attitude toward your children when they disappoint you?

The Christian Woman and Her Children
THE MATURE MOTHER

Only take heed to yourself, and diligently keep yourself, lest you forget the things your eyes have seen, and lest they depart from your heart all the days of your life. And teach them to your children and your grandchildren.
—Deuteronomy 4:9

A mature mother can delay gratifying herself to serve her children.

A STUDENT MAY LEARN in biology classes that almost anyone reaching a certain physical age can become a parent and produce offspring. But only the mentally and emotionally mature can bring them up in such a way that they will grow into good, responsible adults whose lives are a blessing to society, to their parents, and to God.

A mature mother is defined by how far she has come from the stage of immaturity called infancy. Infants want immediate gratification, and they yell and scream until they get it. They respond only to those people who meet their needs, unaware of anyone else's needs. A young child makes decisions on what will be good now, in the short term, without considering the future or long-term view. An immature person will resist something that should be done and instead do something that is desired at the moment.

An emotionally mature mother will be effective in her child's development and spiritual life by her own maturity in these areas. God knows that a woman with no personal experience with Him can't lead her children to have a relationship with God. Modeling His teachings every day and talking of them in the home will lead the children to live them. Fathers and mothers have been given the responsibility for carefully teaching their children and living an exemplary life before them, encouraging them to be strong Christian people.

For Your Reflection

The kind of mother you are or will be from this point on depends upon how mature you are. If becoming more mature has not been your pattern up to now, begin today.

The Christian Woman and Her Children
GOD'S CAPABLE WOMAN

Many daughters have done well, but you excel them all.
—**Proverbs 31:29**

A woman can obey God and leave the consequences to Him.

The Bible provides a detailed description of a capable woman in Proverbs 31:10–31. Although the chapter doesn't say how long she had been married or the ages of her children, it describes her worth to her family, her noble character, and her industrious work on behalf of her family, her household, and the poor. She used money she earned to benefit others and had the respect and love of her husband and children. It appears that she was able to achieve a balance between husband, family, home, and work, and received praise for it. A woman can study this chapter to learn these valuable traits and apply them to her life.

In some parts of the world and/or times in history, there has been controversy about the value of educating daughters for a professional track at college and graduate school, who may become homemakers and mothers. Educating daughters makes sense because there will be some women who do not marry or marry later in life, and they will need marketable skills to provide for themselves. Those who do marry and have children might lose their husbands through accidents or death, and have to bring up children alone. Some women choose to enter the workforce when their children are older and more independent. Some marry a man whose chosen profession doesn't command enough salary to provide for them and they may both work.

An education provides many options for a woman. A career of being a homemaker, wife, and mother requires more training and skills than many professional or licensed jobs. A Christian wife will have to recognize God's perfect will for her life and seek her husband's direction as to how she can balance a husband, home, children, and career/job.

For Your Reflection

As you read Proverbs 31, remember that God promises to give us, day by day, His power and strength to accomplish His will.

The Christian Woman and Her Children
MOTHERS TEACH CHILDREN ABOUT GOD

And these words which I command you today shall be in your heart. You shall teach them diligently to your children, and shall talk of them when you sit in your house, when you walk by the way, when you lie down, and when you rise up.
—DEUTERONOMY 6:6–7

A wife can assist her husband's spiritual training of their children.

IN ANCIENT TIMES, God commanded the Israelites to make a marker of stones at the sites of important historical events. As they passed by these stones the children might have asked, "What do these stones mean?" The fathers would have taught them the history of Israel and all the mighty acts that God had performed on their behalf. The Jewish children grew up knowing God was the subject of each historical marker and of the law, which was read, told, and observed.

God chose Abraham to be the father of the nation of Israel, and through him, God taught many people. "For I have known him, in order that he may command his children and his household after him" (Gen. 18:19). The New Testament tells of the conversion to faith in Christ of two men and records that each was saved and "all his house" (Acts 11:14 and 16:31–34).

The father is responsible to God for the spiritual health of his family. Ideally, he should hold a time of family devotion to God, tell the children Bible stories, pray with them, show them God's unconditional love through his words and actions, and take them regularly to church. If he is unavailable or unwilling to take this responsibility, the mother can assist him in these areas.

A mother can read the Bible to them, teach them to pray, talk with them about God, and convey confidence in His presence. She can organize the family schedule in advance of church services so that the children have had a meal and have clean clothes to wear. As the children get older, she can teach them to schedule a regular time to pray. Her attitude of joy in the Lord will influence their perception of faith.

FOR YOUR REFLECTION

Where is your family lacking in spiritual teaching at home?

The Christian Woman and Her Children
A MOTHER'S SON

> For this child I prayed, and the L ORD has granted me my petition which I asked of Him. Therefore I also have lent him to the L ORD; as long as he lives he shall be lent to the L ORD.
> —1 S AMUEL 1:27–28

A son may try to become everything his mother respects in a man.

A MOTHER CAN SET an example in such a way that her son will choose to become a godly man. The things she appreciates and compliments in her husband and in other men indicate to her son what traits she believes are important. If she is critical of men and her husband in particular, her son may seek to live the feminine role to escape criticism or disapproval. If she is dependent on his father for protection and advice, the son may seek to be knowledgeable and strong, and begin to protect her and his siblings, someday transferring this practice to a healthy protection of his own family. If she is overly protective of her son, he may acquire fear and insecurity, learning to lean on his girlfriend and later, his wife, rather than having women lean on him. A wise mother asks her son to wash and repair the family car, make home repairs, and lead the family in prayer before meals when his father is out of town or has passed away. If he learns to do these things at home, he will gain confidence to do them in his own home after he marries.

There is often a special bond between a mother and a son, and she may have a soft heart toward him. A mother must exercise self-discipline not to interfere as she observes her husband's approach to training him. Fathers will take a hard stand to toughen their sons because a man knows what a boy needs to face the future successfully, and what ways he can prepare him for the day he leaves home. Mothers who show respect for the father are also showing respect for the son.

F OR Y OUR R EFLECTION

Do you use masculine nicknames and adjectives to compliment your son? Do you allow your son to open doors and carry heavy things for you? Do you encourage him to accept challenges? How do you support his father's disciplinary methods?

The Christian Woman and Her Children
MOTHERS ARE NOT PERFECT

And when he is old he will not depart from it.
—Proverbs 22:6

*Mothers can ask for forgiveness when they
have wronged their children.*

IF A MOTHER were to be an example to her children in all things, this would include being an example in the area of repentance and restoration of relationships. When she loses her temper, is unkind, or commits any other sin that she is aware of before the children, she can be quick to explain the blunder, ask for forgiveness, and make an earnest attempt to change for the better, without drawing attention to it afterward. This kind of example teaches the child God's way of meeting the problems of daily living.

A conscientious mother will work hard to bring up her children realizing that no parent is perfect. All fathers and mothers are imperfect parents who disagree with their mates and wrong their children. They accuse them falsely, judge them prematurely, afflict them unjustly, and confuse them unwillingly. If a mother and father humbly seek to obey God's authority, lovingly and consistently correct their children when they fail, and honestly confess their faults, they can influence their children in powerful ways by their example.

Imperfect mothers can nevertheless be godly ones! A mother needs God's help to be obedient to Him, to honor His commands, to have maturity and energy to do her job well. She must do all she can for her children, and then trust God to do His part.

For Your Reflection

How are you increasing your knowledge of God? Do you have a quiet time alone with God each day? Ask Him to forgive you for your trespasses against your children, and to bring all areas of your motherhood under His guidance.

The Christian Woman and Her Children
MOTHERS OF INFANTS

For You formed my inward parts; you covered me in my mother's womb.
—PSALM 139:13

A baby's brain develops rapidly in the womb and after birth.

WHEN A FIRST pregnancy is confirmed, a prospective mother can experience many emotions. Delight, excitement, fear, anxiety, stress, concern, joy, anticipation, worry, awe, and wonder are some. "I'm not ready for this!" or "What do I know about taking care of a baby?" may be some thoughts she has. As the pages are peeled off the calendar and the birth draws nearer, many preparations have been taking place inside the womb.

Inside the womb since conception, the baby's brain develops through a precise network of neurons that begin weaving intricate, coordinated patterns of neural activity. This miraculous process wires the brain for a lifetime of learning and drives the explosion of learning that occurs immediately after birth. It is as if the brain has laid out circuits that are its best guess about what is required for vision, language, and more.

Shortly after birth, the brain produces trillions more connections between the neurons reinforcing connections guessed at, and eliminating others that weren't needed. Those that are impoverished from not being stimulated are eliminated. A baby deprived of stimulating challenges to learn will have a brain that suffers and never fully develops as it could have.

Many couples today are pressed for time and spend more hours away from their baby than with him/her. An infant who is not cuddled, loved, spoken or sung to, accepted, and challenged has a brain that may not develop properly. Challenges given by the parents through interaction with people, toys, music, and other stimuli with assurance of love cause a baby's brain to strengthen, with lifelong results.

∽

FOR YOUR REFLECTION

Do you talk to your baby, smile often, cuddle her, and give her safe places to explore? Are you her primary caregiver? Is there a new mother who needs a mentor as she begins her journey into motherhood?

The Christian Woman and Her Children
MORE MOTHERS OF INFANTS

I will praise You, for I am fearfully and wonderfully made.
—Psalm 139:14

A baby develops healthfully with sensory challenges and love.

An infant gets information about the world through his senses. He will learn, through time and practice, to use them to increase his awareness and to act in logical ways.

He has been hearing his mother's voice before birth. She can continue to talk and sing to him, and mimic his sounds, so that he will learn the beginnings of language. Studies have shown that exposure to classical music develops math readiness.

He can see at birth, but not in close detail until he is several weeks old. A mother can stimulate his sense of sight by looking at him, smiling at him, and using a finger or a rattle in front of his eyes to challenge him to track it with his eyes.

He can smell his mother's breast milk and her body scent after a few weeks. She can place him in a safe place to smell her cooking with different spices and foods.

His movements are uncoordinated and spasmodic at birth, but as he grows, he needs safe places to stretch out on a blanket to see, touch, smell, taste, grab, and hold different objects. Soon he will roll over, creep, and crawl. A mother can dance with her baby, combining music and motion.

Bonding is the two-way relationship between mother and child that develops over the first three years. A baby will learn to trust his mother's ability as she responds to his cues. Trust establishes emotional security, conscience, and empathy in the earliest weeks of life. Therefore, it is essential that an infant be thoughtfully cared for by his mother as much as possible.

For Your Reflection

How are you managing your schedule as a new mother to leave time to spend with your infant? Who is with him while you are away from him? What will you change to be sure he is getting challenged mentally, cuddled, and loved?

The Christian Woman and Her Children
MOTHERS OF CHILDREN

*Even a child is known by his deeds, whether
what he does is pure and right.*
—PROVERBS 20:11

A *mother can lay a foundation of good character in her children.*

A CHRISTIAN MOTHER'S RESPONSIBILITY before the Lord includes raising children of good character. Developing character requires the consistent focus of the parents from birth forward. Some examples are encouraging the wobbly-kneed toddler to continue walking in spite of frustrating falls, giving the older child plenty of opportunities to learn the muscle coordination to run, to balance on a bicycle, and to perfect the butterfly stroke, despite challenges, for the swim team. All of these opportunities are challenges the child faces that lead to the development of not only a strong body, but lay the foundations necessary to develop the character traits of discipline, diligence, long-suffering, and patience.

According to the dictionary, character means, "a distinguishing feature or attribute; moral or ethical strength; integrity; fortitude."[1] A mother can keep this definition in mind as she nurtures and teaches her children.

Biblical character traits include ambition, bravery, chastity, cheerfulness, compassion, contentment, dependability, diligence, discretion, fairness, faithfulness, forgiveness, godliness, graciousness, holiness, honesty, humility, kindness, long-suffering, loving, obedience, patience, prayerful, respectfulness, and truthfulness. These traits can be taught by a loving and consistent example by parents, with repeated encouragement, until the desired outcome is reached.

By-products of developing a godly character would include obeying parents, making wise decisions, problem solving, cleanliness, orderliness, getting along with others, the habit of happiness, and goal setting and attainment.

FOR YOUR REFLECTION

Ask God to build these biblical character traits solidly in your heart and life first, and then in the hearts and lives of each of your children.

The Christian Woman and Her Children
MOTHERS OF TEENS

The effective, fervent prayer of a righteous man avails much.
—James 5:16

A mother can love, affirm, and pray for her teenaged child.

THE TEENAGE YEARS are a time of transition for children from childhood to adulthood. Every teen has hormonal changes in his body that affect skin, energy levels, emotions, and brain activity. Physically, he may seem lazy, but he is growing, and may need more rest. He may have acne, which may not be the result of poor habits, but could be a skin condition requiring a doctor's care. Emotionally, a teen may be experiencing great mood swings. She may be rebellious and independent one moment, and then scared the next. Parents find the erratic behavior challenging and may need to make changes.

A mother carries much of the responsibility of nurturing, teaching, and disciplining young children. When the preteen years appear, it becomes the father's place to assume the bulk of parenting. In addition, both parents will need to agree on and set boundaries, and speak in unison before their teens to enforce them.

Teens, particularly adolescent young men, have a great need to have a vital relationship with their father. Daily quality interaction, affection, and outings together create a strong and stable bond in the father-son relationship. A father may need to rearrange his schedule to focus on the time he will need to forge this relationship with his teen. It will call for some sacrifice for the father to accept this challenge.

A mother can deepen her commitment to pray during these years. She must speak with one voice with her husband to the children, and maintain their unity as parents. Keeping her house organized, having dinner as a family, and creating an atmosphere of unconditional love and acceptance is the simplest way for a mother to navigate the teen years.

FOR YOUR REFLECTION

Keep this formula in mind for teens: Time + Teen + Relationship + Prayer + Unity of Husband and Wife = Progress and Change. Which area is the biggest struggle for you? If you are a single mother, seek to engage your teen's father in making time for him/her.

The Christian Woman and Her Children
THE SINGLE MOTHER

I can do all things through Christ who strengthens me.
—PHILIPPIANS 4:13

A single mother can ask others to help her bring up her child.

A WIDOW, UNMARRIED, OR divorced woman has challenges mothering her child without a husband and father in the home. She can try to establish a biblical line of authority (see Chapter 4) in her family, so that she and her child will be under God's umbrella of protection.

She can reconcile with the child's natural father and seek to be on speaking terms with him. The father should help her financially and attend the child's school programs, athletic events, piano recitals, graduation ceremonies, and other activities of importance to the family. The child will be more secure and less fearful if he has a relationship with his natural father, by spending enjoyable time together regularly.

If possible, she can ask her father or mature brother to model the male role for her child by offering advice and counsel to him, helping learn to repair things in her home, becoming a mentor in his educational pursuits, and giving his perspective on the child's personality and behavior. If no father or brother is available, she could ask if a married couple in the church could fill this role.

The single mother can locate the best job and the best working schedule for her family. She may need to upgrade her skills in order to find employment that has good medical and insurance benefits, and policies that accommodate sick leave for an ill child, or for school functions.

The single mother has many roles such as provider, mother, father, homemaker, and employee. Because of her fatigue and stress, she will need to take care of herself by taking time to pray and attend church, exercising regularly, and getting a good night's sleep. God knows how difficult the world is, and will provide strength for every aspect of her life, including motherhood.

FOR YOUR REFLECTION

If you are a single mother, how does your child see the roles of father and mother reflected in you and those around your home? What can you do to help lighten the burden of a single mother you know?

The Christian Woman and Her Children
THE SINGLE MOTHER AND CHILD CARE

And we know that all things work together for good to those who love God, to those who are the called according to His purpose.
—Romans 8:28

A single mother can make each day enjoyable with her child.

A SINGLE MOTHER CAN seek childcare from relatives, a childcare center, a nanny, or a babysitter. An older child can be left at school to attend enrichment activities, or left alone at home, with strict guidelines. A single mother can combine different kinds of childcare throughout the years that her children need it, weighing the pros and cons, depending on the needs of her family.

Sometimes relatives are trustworthy, willing, and committed to help. The advantages of asking relatives are possible lower costs, more one-on-one attention for the child, less risk of outside influences, and often, similar values and parenting styles.

She can locate the best childcare center in her area. Good library and retail books on this subject and the recommendations of friends will help her to think through and compile a list of questions to ask the staff when she visits the center to observe.

A nanny can be a viable choice if a mother's career requires travel, as she can live in the home with the child. She must be investigated for qualifications such as training, past references, and police records. The same would apply to a babysitter. Either could live in or out of the home. A child must be of legal age according to the local police department to be left alone. She can be left for gradually increasing lengths of time to adjust to this new situation. A kind neighbor can assist with emergencies.

A single mother who needs to find childcare for her child may feel overwhelming feelings of guilt and grieving over what she and her child might have had. However, she can arrange the best care she can and rest assured that she is a good mother for meeting the financial needs of her family by working.

For Your Reflection

If you are a single mother, what kind of childcare arrangement seems to fit the best? As you drop off or leave your child for childcare, ask God to guide and protect his heart and body.

The Christian Woman and Her Children
MOTHER-IN-LAW

Then the women said to Naomi, "Blessed be the L<small>ORD</small>, who has not left you this day without a close relative; and may his name be famous in Israel! And may he be to you a restorer of life and a nourisher of your old age; for your daughter-in-law, who loves you, who is better to you than seven sons, has borne him."
—R<small>UTH</small> 4:14–15

A mother-in-law's goal is to help her child's marriage succeed.

W<small>ITH ALL THE</small> cartoons, jokes, hair-raising tales, and experiences heard and told, it is no wonder that problems exist sometimes between families and mothers-in-law. These women come in all sizes, shapes, personalities, preferences, and skills that enable or disable them to get along with the newest member of the family.

Whether she is married, widowed, or divorced, there are new challenges and opportunities given to the mother-in-law as the new family makes all the required adjustments. She can pray daily for the couple and determine to do all she can to help her child's marriage succeed. It is biblical for her child and his/her mate to become "one flesh." She can be prepared to offer wise counsel and advice when asked. She may want to help the couple, but must discern what is truly helpful and what verges on spoiling, enabling, or interfering.

Grandchildren and step-grandchildren are people God has brought into her life so that she can pray for them and show them by her love and actions that Christ loves them. Her married children have the duty to raise their children as they wish and to honor their parents, but this does not require that either party make daily phone calls and visits.

If she is married, she can concentrate on her own marriage. Whether married or not, she can concentrate on being a good companion, develop deeper communication skills, and enjoy being a good homemaker. Efforts in these areas will help her transition to her new role as mother-in-law.

F<small>OR</small> Y<small>OUR</small> R<small>EFLECTION</small>

Examine yourself and your position with your married child, looking for both positive and negative traits you exhibit that help or hinder his/her marriage success.

The Christian Woman and Her Children
DAUGHTER-IN-LAW

But Ruth said: "Entreat me not to leave you, or to turn back from following after you; for wherever you go, I will go; and wherever you lodge, I will lodge; your people shall be my people, and your God, my God."
—RUTH 1:16

A wife's loyalty to her husband's parents is pleasing to God.

A DAUGHTER-IN-LAW PLEASES HER in-laws by making their son happy. She can seek to be the best companion, helper, and eventually mother she can be, with God's help. It is important that she stays true to herself and develops her own talents in these roles.

The Bible story of Ruth provides real insight about a good relationship between a daughter-in-law and mother-in-law. Ruth (daughter-in-law) demonstrated love, concern, and faithfulness for Naomi (mother-in-law) that was known by the entire community. Her loyalty to Naomi and the laws of God enabled her to meet and marry Boaz, her near kinsman.

A daughter-in-law can spend time getting to know her in-laws through periodic calls, letters, visits, sharing news, and being a good listener. She can do her best to accept some of their family traditions and lifestyle, even though they may be different from hers. After all, they produced a son who is now her husband. Speaking respectfully of him to them, and of them to him and others, will help to create a positive relationship. She can listen willingly and politely to his parents' advice, but she and her husband will need to discuss and decide things for themselves.

When their children are born, each grandchild can be encouraged to have a good relationship with grandparents. When her in-laws become elderly, she and her husband can offer to help them financially or invite them to live in their home.

∽

FOR YOUR REFLECTION

What can you do today to encourage and be a blessing to your in-laws?

The Christian Woman and Her Children
MARRIED DAUGHTERS

Honor your father and your mother, as the LORD *your God has commanded you, that your days may be long, and that it may be well with you in the land which the* LORD *your God is giving you.*
—DEUTERONOMY 5:16

A daughter continues to honor her parents after her marriage.

A MARRIED DAUGHTER CAN concentrate on making her marriage succeed. In order to do this, she will have to leave her parents and cleave to her husband.

Once she has left her parents to form her marriage, it is an adjustment for parents to realize that their daughter is old enough to have her own home. She should assure them of her love and her desire to prove to them that they were good parents. A scriptural attitude of honor for her parents is reflected through her actions to periodically visit, call, write letters, and invite her parents to visit her new home. She may also inquire as to their well-being, and how she may pray for them and their needs.

When her children are born, she can encourage each child to have a good relationship with grandparents. She may realize that they may be used of the Lord to help her child establish faith in Him. Their advice and help is valuable and worth listening to, because it comes from many years of experience as parents. As they become elderly, she and her husband can help them financially, or perhaps ask them to live in their home.

If there are strained relations between her parents (sometimes due to divorce or remarriage), a daughter can keep a good relationship with each person as much as possible. If God is leading, she may talk honestly with the estranged parent, speaking of her own thoughts and feelings, while showing total respect for their position.

FOR YOUR REFLECTION

As a married daughter, how do you honor your parents? What can you do to encourage a good relationship between your children and their grandparents?

The Christian Woman and Her Children
GRANDMOTHERS

Those who are planted in the house of the LORD shall flourish in the courts of our God. They shall still bear fruit in old age; they shall be fresh and flourishing.
—PSALM 92:13–14

Each grandchild is a gift to a grandmother from God.

SOCIETY TODAY IS extremely mobile, with families moving often. While grandparents were once part of the everyday life of a family, now they are often separated from it by hundreds of miles, so effort must be made to be together periodically. The unconditional love, stability, undivided attention, and prayer support a Christian grandmother can give to each grandchild or step-grandchild is highly beneficial to the modern family.

The role of grandmother is an extension of the God-given drive to be a mother. As a woman receives the gift of a grandchild, she may see him or her as an opportunity for growth and adventure. Some suggestions and tips on the following pages offer ways to enjoy grandchildren and to be a good influence on them.

She may be a grandmother to natural grandchildren or step-grandchildren. Some grandmothers today are bringing up their grandchildren, as young mothers remain in the workplace and need daycare for their children. There are also grandparents bringing up grandchildren because the real parents want to escape the responsibility.

FOR YOUR REFLECTION

What is your attitude toward being an older woman and a grandmother? What do you hope the effects of your role will be on your children and grandchildren?

The Christian Woman and Her Children
GRANDMOTHERS AND NATURAL GRANDCHILDREN

I thank God, whom I serve with a pure conscience, as my forefathers did, as without ceasing I remember you in my prayers night and day, greatly desiring to see you, being mindful of your tears, that I may be filled with joy, when I call to remembrance the genuine faith that is in you, which dwelt first in your grandmother Lois and your mother Eunice, and I am persuaded is in you also.
—2 Timothy 1:3–5

Grandmothers can build a relationship with each grandchild.

A GRANDMOTHER CAN PRAY for each grandchild daily that he will be a Christian and grow into maturity with the Lord Jesus Christ. She can teach him to be obedient and respectful to God, his parents, and other authorities as she reads the Bible to him (Deut. 6:6–9). She can explain God's love and special plan for him.

Since grandchildren come in all different forms and personalities, she can observe and seek to understand each one's particular bent, loving and accepting them as they are, and helping where she can, to strengthen areas found wanting.

To build an enjoyable relationship with each grandchild, she can spend time with him. Attending sporting events, musicals, libraries, museums, or amusement parks builds happy memories. Going hiking or fishing, or taking him on vacation, allows each of them to get to know one another. When he visits her home, she can help him develop adult skills such as repairing items, woodworking, fixing cars, gardening, and managing finances. A granddaughter may not have learned in her home to cook, bake, sew, or develop hobbies like quilting, scrapbooking, gardening, or knitting, and a grandmother has the time and skills to teach her.

It is important for a grandmother to respect the boundaries of her role by realizing that she is not the parent. She can communicate often and openly with the parents, but avoid taking sides when turmoil comes.

For Your Reflection

In what ways is your role as a grandmother a benefit to your grandchild?

The Christian Woman and Her Children
GRANDMOTHERS AND STEP-GRANDCHILDREN

A merry heart makes a cheerful countenance, but by sorrow of the heart the spirit is broken.
—PROVERBS 15:13

Grandmothers can help provide stability for step-grandchildren.

A STEP-GRANDCHILD IS A victim of circumstances not of her own making and she may feel that she is caught in crossfire between two families. She may be living in separate homes with each parent for specified periods of time. She may be getting to know new relatives. The divorce may have required relocation, a new school, and new friends. She may be experiencing emotional traumas and new pressures that she is unable to express in words. Her feelings may be reflected in erratic behavior that varies from being cooperative to rebellious. These life changes will require all of her energy to manage.

A grandmother of such a step-grandchild can provide some stability in an unstable situation. She may be the only one who is objective, emotionally steady, supportive, a prayer warrior, and a good example. She can listen, but it would be unwise for her to question the step-grandchild for information, or to speak unkindly about any family members. She can discuss with the parents what name the grandchild should call her, realizing that allowing her to be called by her first name takes away some of the authority that usually goes with "grandmother."

Keeping up a cheerful and positive countenance, helping her step-grandchild to see another side of life, rather than just her particular view, will help to forge a new, positive relationship.

FOR YOUR REFLECTION

How can you and your step-grandchild benefit from your relationship?

The Christian Woman and Her Children
GRANDMOTHERS BRINGING UP GRANDCHILDREN

That you may fear the LORD your God, to keep all His statutes and His commandments which I command you, you and your son and your grandson, all the days of your life, and that your days may be prolonged.
—DEUTERONOMY 6:2

God can be trusted to assist grandparents to bring up grandchildren.

SOMETIMES A CHILD has been left to his grandparents to be brought up because his parents died, divorced, were mentally or physically ill, or just irresponsible. As difficult and unexpected as this situation sometimes is, God can be trusted to assist grandparents to succeed.

It is important to establish God's line of authority in the family (see Chapter 4) and to expect obedience from the grandchild. If this is to be a permanent arrangement, he can be expected to have chores and responsibilities around the house, rules with appropriate consequences, discipline with love, and encouragement to be obedient to God. Church youth functions will provide opportunities to establish quality friendships, and grandmothers will want to know his friends and where he is at all times.

If the grandmother is the main caregiver due to her child's irresponsibility, she can make an objective evaluation of her parenting style. She may be partially responsible for some of her child's behavior, such as how she has learned to make choices, the way she handled stress and responsibility, or how to love another person. A grandmother can pray about and then list some of the ways she can do things differently with this generation.

FOR YOUR REFLECTION

How can you encourage faith in your grandchild? Some promises to encourage you as you bring up your grandchild can be found in the following verses: Isaiah 40:28–29, and 46:4. See also Psalm 102:17 and Lamentations 2:19.

CHAPTER 6

THE CHRISTIAN WOMAN AND HOME MANAGEMENT

The Christian Woman and Home Management
HOME MANAGEMENT

*The wise woman builds her house, but the
foolish pulls it down with her hands.*
—Proverbs 14:1

Home management can be a woman's mission and ministry for God.

HOME MANAGEMENT IS the oldest, most revered profession for women. To be a good home manager, a woman must have more knowledge, expend more physical energy, and be proficient in a greater number of different skills than in many professions and licensed jobs. Bookkeeping, purchasing, budgeting, gardening, interior decorating, and cleaning would name a few of the many skills of home manager. If she is a wife and mother, childbearing, child development, counseling, nutrition, and nursing can be added to the list.

Home management is a *career*, a chosen pursuit, and lifework. A homemaker is defined in the dictionary as "a person who manages a household; especially, a housewife."[1] Managing a household has as much challenge and opportunity, success and failure, growth, expansion and incentives as any corporate career, and requires the same dedication, hard work, and creativity.

Good home management skills are imperative for a stable marriage relationship. Unless the home is kept clean and orderly enough to make both husband and wife comfortable, there can be trouble. A well-kept home is a haven for family, friends, and strangers, and a setting to offer hospitality to all.

Many examples are given in the Bible of women with whom God was pleased, and in most of these accounts, the home was their main sphere of service to Him. The woman described in Proverbs 31 was motivated to efficiently run her household and care for her family out of reverence for God.

FOR YOUR REFLECTION

Study the woman described in Proverbs 31:10–31. List the tasks this woman did that you would define for yourself as being your responsibility. How can you develop or refine skills and excel in these areas?

The Christian Woman and Home Management
A WORKING ATTITUDE

I do not pray that You should take them out of the world, but that You should keep them from the evil one. They are not of the world, just as I am not of the world.
—John 17:15–16

Attitudes about homemaking are often shaped by social influences.

As long as Christians are living on the earth, they will be subjected to the influences of the world. The Lord Jesus had this in mind when He prayed His great intercessory prayer in John 17. He knew that relatives, friends, and neighbors would influence His followers with godless philosophies, so He prayed that God would help them live in the world and be kept from Satan.

Today through the media, Christian women are bombarded continually with philosophies that originate in the minds of those who have not been made new creatures in Christ (2 Cor. 5:17). Women are taught that biblical standards and roles have been discarded and there is now freedom for a woman to choose her own role and moral standards, believing she can have it all, with little regard to what God considers acceptable. These attitudes appeal to a woman's pride in her intelligence and education, and may cause her to think that God's plan for women to be good home managers may be outdated, unnecessary, and beneath her dignity. It is important that she have the opportunity to contrast these thoughts with biblical truth and a commitment to follow Christ.

Her attitude toward being a home manager is also shaped by her mother's example. A mother shapes a young girl's attitude toward homemaking in several ways: she has a good or poor relationship with her husband that influences her motivation to keep her house in good order; she enjoys or is bored by homemaking; she stays home to work or works away from home, affecting the energy and time that she can devote to home management. Perhaps a daughter helps with the housework with a positive attitude or she is forced to do much of it because her mother is unavailable. The influence of godless philosophies and childhood memories affect a woman's confidence as a home manager.

For Your Reflection

Whose example will you emulate in managing your home?

The Christian Woman and Home Management
LOVE YOUR NEIGHBOR

> *Jesus said to him, "'You shall love the Lord your God with all your heart, with all your soul, and with all your mind.' This is the first and great commandment. And the second is like it: 'You shall love your neighbor as yourself.'"*
> —Matthew 22:37–39

A homemaker loves her neighbors by ministering to them.

MANAGING A HOUSEHOLD requires an unselfish attitude toward others. A woman may at any time have a husband, family, roommate, relative, church member, or friend living in her home. Any one of them would be her neighbor. She prepares and offers food and drink, invites others into her home, clothes them, nurses them, and keeps them company. To work continuously at mundane and repetitive tasks for neighbors who are sometimes difficult and ungrateful requires an unselfish attitude.

The woman in whom God delights willingly gets out of bed before she wants to in the morning, cooks breakfast for others, makes the same beds she made yesterday, picks up the things others should not have left out, shops in the crowded markets, waits in lines, drives others to and fro, is home and has a meal ready when others are ready to eat, bathes children, cares for the elderly and the ill, sews, does the laundry, and many other services only to begin again the next day. A selfish woman has a small chance of being happy in this role of service to others.

A Christian woman obeys the great command given by Jesus in the opening verse, to "Love your neighbor as yourself" (Matt. 22:39) through her rewarding role as a home manager. Dorothy Patterson, contributing author of the book, *Recovering Biblical Manhood and Womanhood*, has said: "Few women realize what great service they are doing for humanity and for the kingdom of Christ when they provide a haven for the family, the foundation on which all else is built."[1]

∾

For Your Reflection

What areas of home management are difficult for you? Will you consider reading books or seeking the advice of your mother or a friend who can help you with these areas of difficulty?

The Christian Woman and Home Management
COMPETENT PROFESSIONALS

She watches over the ways of her household, and does not eat the bread of idleness.
—Proverbs 31:27

The contented home manager sees her daily work as a profession.

ONCE A WOMAN regards her profession as a home manager as God's high calling for her, she will approach her career as any professional would and look for ways to build her skills and expertise. She will look at the areas where she needs improvement, such as time management, cooking, grocery shopping, home decorating, sewing, laundry and ironing, gardening, or crafts. She can take college courses, read articles and books, watch educational television programs, and ask friends and family to teach her. Knowledge and ability is gained through continued education and daily application of three skills. First there is *planning*, second is *organization*, and third is *self-discipline*.

Planning involves making long-range plans, monthly plans, weekly plans, and daily plans. Plans are kept in a calendar, which can be in a handheld device, a computer, or a notebook—all preferably portable. There are excellent time management seminars, tutorials, and books available along with planning tools that can be purchased.

Organization puts these plans into a logical, orderly progression. Before a woman starts the day, she can make a list of tasks to be accomplished in the home such as cooking, planning daily menus, cleaning, errands, learning a new homemaking skill, personal time, and helping others. As she completes each task on her list, she sees her progress throughout the day.

Self-discipline requires a woman to be a person of action instead of intent. Setting a timer and completing a task in the allotted time motivates her to start. Following each work time slot with something pleasant for her, such as a walk or phoning a friend, keeps her on task. Over time, the satisfaction of seeing her work done and the compliments she receives from others will motivate her to repeat these tasks again without as much hesitation.

FOR YOUR REFLECTION

How can you be creative in every area of your home?

The Christian Woman and Home Management
TEACHING YOUNGER WOMEN

That they admonish the young women to love their husbands, to love their children, to be discreet, chaste, homemakers, good, obedient to their own husbands, that the word of God may not be blasphemed.
—Titus 2:4–5

An older Christian woman can teach a younger woman.

THE HOME SHOULD be the first place where a girl can begin preparing herself toward excellence in the field of homemaking. A mother can help her learn not only how to do these things, but to excel in them. If she is teaching her daughter to sew, set the table, iron clothes, wash dishes, shop wisely, treat minor illnesses, and make her room pretty, she should give her compliments so that she can know some satisfaction for a job done well.

Girls learn from a mother's example and exposure to homemaking tasks as they grow up. Unwise parents do the work themselves because it seems easier than teaching, being patient, repeating instructions, and giving praise. Some parents think that the schools will teach life skills in home economics class, but many schools have removed these classes from their curriculum. The home is the most important training ground for marriage, where young people get their view of the role that they must fulfill in the marriage relationship, and how they want their homes to be.

Christian women can be available to the young girls and women of their church to help them build confidence in homemaking skills they will need, whether or not they marry. They may invite them into their homes to show them what a warm, clean, organized home looks like. They may serve them a meal at a dining room table with flowers, cloth napkins, and freshly prepared food, using plates, utensils, and glasses. Proper etiquette can be practiced, such as serving and passing food, use of utensils, and dining manners so that they can learn the art of hospitality. Older women can use this time to show younger women their own housekeeping tips, decorating and gardening ideas, and the loving hand of friendship.

FOR YOUR REFLECTION

What homemaking tasks can you share with your daughter? Does your church need an older woman to teach the younger women?

The Christian Woman and Home Management
HOSPITALITY

Be kindly affectionate to one another with brotherly love, in honor giving preference to one another; not lagging in diligence, fervent in spirit, serving the Lord; rejoicing in hope, patient in tribulation, contributing steadfastly in prayer; distributing to the needs of the saints, given to hospitality.
—ROMANS 12:10–13

A woman's home is a place for practicing her faith.

ACCORDING TO WEBSTER'S Dictionary, hospitality is receiving and entertaining guests in a friendly, generous manner. Christian men and women are commanded in the Holy Scriptures to be hospitable to each other, to the poor, the disabled, and strangers of the household of faith. Inviting friends, brothers, relatives, or neighbors into your home is hospitality, but not particularly Christian hospitality. Jesus commands that those who cannot reciprocate be invited. He promises that the hospitable will be blessed and rewarded by Him (Luke 14:12–14).

Some couples invite visiting pastors, newcomers to the church, the unemployed, those who are lonely, and those who are suffering loss and in need of companionship, as houseguests. The Christian woman who seeks to obey God by being hospitable will realize that He has given her a home and each thing in it, and will dedicate it all back to Him to use as He sees fit. Her good homemaking skills will stretch to serve others outside her family.

Homemaking and hospitality may seem like insurmountable tasks, but God knows this part of her role will give a woman satisfaction and fulfillment. He can work through her in this area to be a blessing to others.

FOR YOUR REFLECTION

Are there lonely, suffering people that you are aware of who need your fellowship and a meal? Sometimes a sick person cannot reciprocate your hospitality, but would appreciate homemade soup delivered by you to his/her home.

CHAPTER 7
THE CHRISTIAN WOMAN HERSELF

The Christian Woman Herself
A PICTURE OF BEAUTY

Being confident of this very thing, that He who has begun a good work in you will complete it until the day of Jesus Christ.
—PHILIPPIANS 1:6

God has provided the way to salvation through Jesus Christ.

Adam and Eve died spiritually in the Garden of Eden by choosing to obey the serpent, rather than God. God promised them a Savior, who would redeem them from spiritual death and give them new life (Gen. 3:15). The focus of the people in the Old Testament was on the Savior. When Jesus the Savior came, He explained to Nicodemus that he must be "born again" (spiritually) in order to be right with God. Jesus was speaking of man's spirit, once dead from sin, coming to life again through His sacrificial death and resurrection to life.

A woman can learn how her spirit can be born by reading God's plan of salvation found in the Scriptures. The apostle Paul said, "that if you confess with your mouth the Lord Jesus and believe in your heart that God has raised Him from the dead, you will be saved" (Rom. 10:9). Jesus emphasized the importance of baptism as a requirement of His disciples: "Go therefore and make disciples of all the nations, baptizing them in the name of the Father and of the Son and of the Holy Spirit, teaching them to observe all things that I have commanded you; and lo, I am with you always, even to the end of the age" (Matt. 28:19–20).

Once a woman has turned to Jesus Christ, accepted Him as her Savior, and been baptized, she is God's picture of beauty because her sins have been forgiven, she has peace with God, and her spirit has come to life. She can then observe all of Jesus's commands, trusting in His promise to be with her.

For Your Reflection

Will you commit yourself to Christ for the first time or renew your commitment?

The Christian Woman Herself
INNER BEAUTY

So we are always confident, knowing that while we are at home in the body we are absent from the Lord. For we walk by faith, not by sight. We are confident, yes, well pleased rather to be absent from the body and to be present with the Lord.
—2 Corinthians 5:6–8

A woman's inner beauty begins with inner dependence.

THERE IS A person, the real self, hiding inside every woman. Her body, what she sees when she looks in the mirror, is the house where her real self lives. Someday that outside part will drop off and her real self will go to meet God. In the above passage, the apostle Paul spoke of his body as the house where he lived. But when he would be present with the Lord, he would be absent from his physical body. The first part of the Christian woman to be made beautiful is the inner part, the real self.

Inner beauty begins with inner dependence. Western society looks up to and respects women who are independent. Many times women leaders are ones who are busy night and day, and give the impression that they need no one: God, their spouse, or other people. Furthermore, they may be proud that they need no one! But according to several Bible passages, God's smiling approval is upon a woman who has a meek and quiet spirit, which implies peace and inner strength. This comes only through dependence. This inner strength is God's will for a woman, and it will come through learning how to draw it from God as she depends, first of all upon Him; secondly, upon her husband; and thirdly, upon other members of the Christian community.

FOR YOUR REFLECTION

How would you describe a woman who possesses inner beauty? What characteristics does she possess? Would you choose to be a dependent or independent woman? What influences have caused you to prefer one or the other?

The Christian Woman Herself
INNER BEAUTY AND DEPENDENCE UPON GOD

Do not let your adornment be merely outward...rather let it be the hidden person of the heart, with the incorruptible beauty of a gentle and quiet spirit, which is very precious in the sight of God.
—1 Peter 3:3–4

A woman cannot possess inner beauty with a sinful heart.

MANY WOMEN ATTEND church, read the Bible occasionally, and pray when they are in trouble, but they have no assurance that God hears their prayers nor do they feel any closeness to God. Some think that they will probably go to heaven, but don't know why. In order for a woman to be assured that she is a Christian, she must consider the facts of the Holy Scriptures and believe them.

When a woman believes Jesus Christ as the Savior and the only way to eternal life with God, her sinful heart is replaced with a new, clean heart, and she is beautiful inside. Following her belief in Him, she must make a profession of faith (Rom. 10:9–10) and be baptized. There are many scriptures that support Jesus's command to baptize believers (Rom. 6:3–5; Mark 1:9–11; 16:16). The Holy Spirit dwells within her and the Bible takes on new meaning, because He enables her to understand it. As she yields to Him, He promises to produce in her the characteristics associated with the life of Jesus. These are listed as love, joy, peace, long-suffering, kindness, goodness, faithfulness, gentleness, and self-control (Gal. 5:22–23).

A Christian woman is dependent on God for her life in Christ. Beginning each day with prayer, asking God's help for the activities that await her and spending time quietly in His presence will deepen a woman's dependence on God. As He changes her nature into gentleness and meekness, she will learn to trust Him by being dependent on others.

For Your Reflection

Jesus Christ came to seek those who had strayed from God and lost their way. Are you lost and looking for God? He is seeking you (Luke 19:1–10). How will you respond to Him?

The Christian Woman Herself
INNER BEAUTY AND PEACE WITH GOD

And the peace of God, which surpasses all understanding, will guard your hearts and minds through Christ Jesus.
—PHILIPPIANS 4:7

Inner beauty is the presence of Christ in a woman's heart.

A PROMINENT THEOLOGIAN ONCE remarked that each person is born with a God-shaped void that can only be filled by Him. In the Bible, people can read that they find peace with God only when they accept the provision God made for them through His Son, Jesus Christ. Therefore, the emptiness a woman feels can only be filled by the presence of Christ in her heart.

After a woman has found peace *with* God, then she can begin to address the areas of her life where she does not yet know the peace *of* God. In the unrest of today, the lack of peace can be a symptom of disobedience to God and His divine plan for a woman.

Obedience to God is the secret of finding peace. The feelings of discontent, restlessness, turmoil, strife, and tension are often caused by failing to do what is right. Sometimes a woman has done the right things in her role, but she has accomplished it by self-effort, which causes her to feel frustration and martyrdom, rather than peace. When a woman allows Christ to work *through* her, she will display a quietness of spirit and peace, and her activity will be lighthearted and Spirit-controlled.

Challenges to inner peace are daily opportunities to trust in Christ. A woman today can be fearful of old age, loneliness, poverty, her children's future, and catastrophic world events. Who but the Lord Jesus Christ can quiet these fears and give peace?

> You will keep him in perfect peace, whose mind is stayed on You, because he trusts in You.
> —ISAIAH 26:3

FOR YOUR REFLECTION

Have you made your peace with God through believing in His Son, Jesus Christ? If so, what anxieties are keeping you from the peace of God? Have you told Him what is bothering you and asked Him for what you need?

The Christian Woman Herself
INNER BEAUTY AND INNER JOY

Until now you have asked nothing in My name. Ask,
and you will receive, that your joy may be full.
—John 16:24

A woman's inner joy is not dependent on her circumstances.

Obedience to God not only brings peace, but also joy. Joy is not dependent on outward circumstances, but upon a spiritual relationship with God. Joy is one of the fruits of the Holy Spirit, something that is given by God to a Christian as she walks with Him (Gal. 5:22). Joy is lasting, while happiness is fleeting because it is dependent on immediate circumstances.

God gives His joy when a Christian woman reads of His promises stated in the Bible: of the plan that He made for her salvation and her eternal home with Him; of His perfect character, which never changes; and of His assurance that He will always be with her. Joy comes when she prays for some person or for some situation, and she hears that the prayer has been answered. A Christian woman derives joy from serving others, by helping them, teaching them, or just being with someone who is hurting and needs a friend.

Joy does not come only as a result of spiritual things like the Bible, prayer, and Christian service. One woman found that the secret of joy was her daily tasks in the home. As she nursed her baby, she prayed, committing the day and her activities to the Lord. As she did the dishes, she meditated on a Bible verse propped on the windowsill. She prayed for each person as she ironed his clothes or cleaned his room.

Throughout the day, as God was part of each task, she learned how to pray without ceasing, walk in fellowship with God, and do all her work "as unto the Lord." She realized that joy was not found in things or circumstances, but in the reward God gives for those who diligently seek Him. Joy is a gift implanted by the Holy Spirit in a Christian woman.

For Your Reflection

Is there an absence of joy and peace in your life? If so, remember that the fruit of the Holy Spirit follows dependence on God.

The Christian Woman Herself
INNER BEAUTY AND DEPENDENCE ON HUSBANDS

Wives, likewise, be submissive to your own husbands, that even if some do not obey the word, they, without a word, may be won by the conduct of their wives, when they observe your chaste conduct accompanied by fear.
—1 Peter 3:1–2

A woman's faith makes it possible to depend on her husband.

WHEN A WOMAN learns dependence on God for everything, it releases her from the compulsion to control her husband and all the circumstances of her home. When it becomes a reality to her that God is in control of every single thing in her life, it gives her the faith she needs to really learn to be submissive to her husband, as required in the opening verses.

It is sometimes easy to seem outwardly dependent upon a husband. She may depend upon him to maintain the car, handle the trash, take care of the property, do home repairs, and even to help discipline the children. But outward dependence is different than inner dependence. A woman can outwardly depend upon her husband, but at the same time retain an attitude of inner independence from him.

God intended marriage to be a picture to the world of Christ's relationship with His Church—a complete, personal, and sacrificial commitment to each other. Some Christian women may balk at submitting to their non-Christian husbands. God commands they do so in order that he may be won—not by nagging, but by holy living. Submission to the husband is the means God uses to win a non-Christian man to Christ in His time.

How can a woman develop a mature dependence on her husband? She can acknowledge aloud to him and to others how much she needs him. When she wants to buy or to change something, she can ask his permission or advice. When she feels like crying, she can cry on his shoulder. If she learns to depend on her husband, she will experience mutual respect, problems will be shared rather than hers alone, and her appreciation of him will grow.

For Your Reflection

Do you depend on God? How do you depend on your husband?

The Christian Woman Herself
INNER BEAUTY AND DEPENDENCE ON OTHERS

And if one member suffers, all the members suffer with it; or if one member is honored, all the members rejoice with it.
—1 Corinthians 12:26

A Christian woman is dependent on other church members.

Christ likens His body, the Church, to a living body made up of different parts (1 Cor. 12:12–31). If the body were made up of only eyes or only arms, it would be incomplete and dysfunctional. All kinds of people make up the Church to be a complete, functioning unit. God did not intend for His children to be independent of Him or of each other.

A Christian woman can develop spiritual interdependence on others. When she is responsible for a project in church, she can let others do their share of the work. If she insists on doing it all herself, others may feel unwanted and unneeded. There are times when she feels depressed, is ill, or even needs to be hospitalized. When others offer to keep her company, cook a meal, or visit her, she should allow them to help her and be thankful. Prayer with others opens friendships. She can ask a friend to share prayer requests, or to simply pray with her in person or over the telephone.

Once a Christian woman establishes the habit of being dependent on God, her husband, and others, a result can be peace. This kind of inner peace is the goal of many people. But it is only to be found when a woman is in the center of God's will.

For Your Reflection

When one of your Christian brothers or sisters suffers, how do you care for and empathize with the hurting member? How do you respond to others' offers to help you when you are suffering?

The Christian Woman Herself
OUTER BEAUTY

*Every way of a man is right in his own
eyes, but the L*ORD *weighs the hearts.*
—PROVERBS 21:2

*Be diligent to present yourself approved to God, a worker who
does not need to be ashamed, rightly dividing the word of truth.*
—2 TIMOTHY 2:15

A woman's outer beauty reflects her attitude.

JUST AS INNER beauty has several components, so does outer beauty. Outer beauty confines itself to three areas: attitude, appearance, and actions. The word *attitude* is defined as "a state of mind or feeling with regard to some matter; disposition."[1] A Christian woman's attitudes will be reflected in how she looks.

During the last hundred years, women have been faced with circumstances and philosophies that have altered their thought patterns. The right to vote, the privilege of higher education, and the changing role of women have presented many challenges to biblical attitudes. Many women have turned from joy in their roles in the home to questioning them and feeling discontented.

Since attitude is reflected in appearance and actions, a woman should consider first what God wants her attitude to be. A personal study of God's attitude toward women and His direct instructions to them can be studied one book of the Bible at a time, noting when and how women are mentioned. She can study each woman of the Bible, noting her situation and God's approval or disapproval of her attitude. As a woman learns God's precepts and applies them to her life, experiencing success, her looks will reflect her transformed thinking and emotions.

∽

FOR YOUR REFLECTION

What mental picture do you have of yourself? What has shaped your attitude?

The Christian Woman Herself
OUTER BEAUTY AND APPEARANCE

*In like manner also, that the women adorn themselves
in modest apparel, with propriety and moderation.*
—1 Timothy 2:9

A woman's appearance can be feminine, stylish, and modest.

Millions of dollars are spent by women per year at cosmetics counters, in beauty salons, and in department stores. The cosmetic industry introduces new products daily that are designed to make a woman look beautiful and smell good. Fashion, hair, and beauty stylists examine pictures from the past to create "new looks" or revive old ones, in an effort to develop the latest image for women.

There are some Christian women who shun material things and embrace a dull appearance, wearing drab colors, shapeless clothes, mostly trousers, no makeup, and/or no jewelry. Some believe this is a godly response to vanity. However, there is no biblical precedent for this. Others dress sensually and excessively, imitating the immodest and vulgar fashions so often paraded by the fashion magazines and movie stars, and seem unaware of their value as Christian women of influence in a depraved culture.

A woman should take the time daily to bathe, wear makeup, style her hair, and dress attractively and properly for the occasions of her life. Her beauty affects her mental attitude toward herself and her daily tasks. Her husband, boyfriend, brother, boss, store clerks, and anyone who comes into her daily presence are all positively affected by her smile, and feminine, stylish, and modest dress.

A Christian woman will begin with inner beauty, tending her spirit with Scripture, prayer, and praise. From there, she will dress the body that houses her inner beauty, and then move out into her life with beautiful action!

For Your Reflection

What do you need to change to have an attractive appearance? How will it affect you and others that you encounter daily?

The Christian Woman Herself
OUTER BEAUTY AND COUNTENANCE

*Let your light so shine before men, that they may see
your good works and glorify your Father in heaven.*
—MATTHEW 5:16

A woman's feminine and gracious countenance glorifies God.

GOD WANTS EVERY Christian to be careful how he or she lives—concentrating on good works and service that will glorify God. Sometimes in doing good, a Christian is criticized. Perhaps it is not the good works that are criticized, but the way in which they are done.

Christian womanhood implies that a woman's actions be womanly as well as Christian. It is important to greet people warmly, but they can be offended if a woman behaves like a man and slaps them on the back, talks to them loudly, or shakes their hands too long or too roughly. If a woman makes a suggestion to another that will help in their work, she must do so in a meek and quiet manner. She speaks to others with wisdom and kindness (Prov. 31:26).

A woman may need to evaluate her life to see if her actions and intentions are Christian, but not womanly or feminine. One of these areas is her physical bearing. She can walk lightly with good posture. Modesty requires that when a woman sits, she keep her knees together, with legs crossed at the ankles, not knees. She can get into and out of a car gracefully by sitting first, then bringing her legs into (or out of) the car with her knees together. Graceful hand gestures leave no room for touching her hair or face, pulling at clothing, or applying makeup in public. A pleasing pitch and volume to her voice can be attained with practice, such as answering the telephone with a smile.

God has built a picture of what the ideal woman could be from His point of view in the Bible. Each of His points merits consideration. A Christian woman can reach the goal of being her best for the Lord, her husband, and her children—inside and outside.

∽

FOR YOUR REFLECTION

How can you become more feminine in your speech and actions?

CHAPTER 8

THE CHRISTIAN WOMAN, HER CHURCH AND OTHER ACTIVITIES

The Christian Woman, Her Church and Other Activities
CHURCH AND ACTIVITIES

There is a difference between a wife and a virgin. The unmarried woman cares about the things of the Lord, that she may be holy both in body and in spirit. But she who is married cares about the things of the world—how she may please her husband.
—1 Corinthians 7:34

A wife's ministry at home should take priority over her outside activities.

God has established the Church and given instructions for how it is to function. His plan is orderly and specific for each Christian man and woman. The basic principles guiding a Christian woman's relationship to the Church can also be applied to her other activities which involve both men and women.

There will be a difference in the relationship to the Church between a single woman and a married woman. A married woman has a husband to whom Christ has commanded her to be in submission. The apostle Paul states that a married woman will seek to please her husband. He will be her top priority along with children and their home. If these duties are regularly neglected because of outside activities, disorder in the marriage could result. It is difficult for a man to accept little time and energy from his wife gracefully, without resenting it. It is natural for him to assume that his wife will give him, their home, and children her undivided focus. If a wife considers serving the Lord by working in the Church, she must have a thriving ministry at home first. An unmarried woman submits to Christ as her head. She is free to give undivided focus to Him and His Church. However, all of the instructions the Scriptures give for how a woman relates to the Church will apply to her.

For Your Reflection

How is your calendar of activities reflecting your belief in God's design for women in the Church? What activities are robbing you of energy to care for your husband (if married) or to serve Christ (if unmarried)?

The Christian Woman, Her Church and Other Activities
A WIFE'S RELATIONSHIP TO THE CHURCH

This is a faithful saying: If a man desires the position of a bishop, he desires a good work.
—1 Timothy 3:1

Let deacons be the husbands of one wife, ruling their children and their own houses well.
—1 Timothy 3:12

A wife's attitude will help her husband qualify for church leadership.

The Bible has explicit instructions concerning who should hold authoritative positions in the Church. Qualifications are given for a man who wants to be a bishop, minister, or a deacon. Leadership within a family is vested in the husband and father, and the Church, as God's household, requires wise and competent leadership by men. Women are not to be in authoritative roles in the Church because such a position would not be consistent with God's role for her in marriage as established at Creation as the submissive partner.

Churches that do not follow biblical instructions for male leadership allow women to serve in roles assigned to men. If women continue to usurp authority because it is possible and because it seems no man wants to lead, men will withdraw and soon the Church could become an organization for women and children.

In any age, the Church functions best in reaching the community by following God's design with men as leaders. Men will become involved and stay in churches where they are the authorities, but will avoid those churches and organizations run by women. Because God created men to lead women, it is most difficult for men to be led by women.

Chapter 3 of 1 Timothy gives many qualifications for men who would like to be leaders in the Church. A wife who is reverent, submissive, and encourages her husband to lead the family will help him to lead in the Church as he does his home.

For Your Reflection

It will take faith and God's strength to resist the unscriptural teachings and actions regarding leadership of the Church today. How will you demonstrate that you are willing to obey God's Word?

The Christian Woman, Her Church and Other Activities
SUBMISSIVE CONDUCT IN CHURCH

Judge among yourselves. Is it proper for a woman to pray to God with her head uncovered? Does not even nature itself teach you that if a man has long hair, it is a dishonor to him? But if a woman has long hair, it is a glory to her; for her hair is given to her for a covering.
—1 Corinthians 11:13–15

A wife's conduct in the Church reflects her submission to her husband.

A WOMAN IS INSTRUCTED to be careful how she conducts herself in the Church, not always doing what comes naturally to her, but learning and applying skills that are commanded by God.

The apostle Paul wrote to the church at Corinth in answer to a letter he had received from them with questions concerning Christian conduct in the community and church there. Some of the problems that transpired were caused by the behavior of the Christian women in the Corinthian church. It seems that they were praying and prophesying with uncovered heads or shorn hair. He admonished them to honor God's order of the sexes in creation and retain some visible sign that they did so. Head coverings or longer hair would distinguish the woman from the man and symbolize her submission to him.

The attitude of submission to God's line of authority is required of both sexes, yet many women think erroneously that submission equals inferiority and precludes equality. Is this true of the Lord Jesus Christ who submitted Himself to His Father's will?

What is applicable from this instruction to women in the Church today? Everything! God's line of authority has not changed. In this day, it is sound advice for a woman to be in submission to her male leaders by deferring to them in all areas of the Church.

For Your Reflection

If you are asked to serve in your church, how does your husband factor in to your decision? How do you demonstrate your awareness of him as your spiritual head?

The Christian Woman, Her Church and Other Activities
SILENT CONDUCT IN THE CHURCH

Let your women keep silent in the churches, for they are not permitted to speak; but they are to be submissive, as the law also says. And if they want to learn something, let them ask their own husbands at home; for it is shameful for women to speak in church.
—1 Corinthians 14:34–35

A woman's silence in church reflects submission to God.

A WOMAN IS INSTRUCTED to be silent while attending church services. Some of the Corinthian women believed that since they had been endowed as equal partners with men in the gift of faith in Christ, and given a gift of the Holy Spirit, such as speaking in tongues or prophesying, that they were exceptions to this rule. The apostle Paul plainly reprimanded them. The woman is instructed not to interrupt the minister or male teacher during church activities. When she has a comment or a question, she is not to speak there, but may discuss anything with her husband at home, or if she is single, she may ask the minister at a time when he is not leading the church service. This instruction to the women would prevent disorder in church.

Today, a wife who is married to a husband who is not a Christian may wonder how she can apply this Scripture verse. A husband seems to have answers for his wife's questions about what is taught in church, and if not, he may find that his interest is piqued in spiritual matters by her asking for his help. She can consult an older churchwoman who should be able to listen and provide direction. A married deacon or minister and his wife can be approached as a couple to provide counsel on spiritual problems.

For Your Reflection

Have you asked your husband spiritual questions recently? How is your conduct in church services and Sunday school? Do you whisper to him during the church service? Do you interrupt, correct, or qualify his remarks when you are in church?

The Christian Woman, Her Church and Other Activities
TEACHING OTHER WOMEN

> *The older women likewise, that they be reverent in behavior, not slanderers, not given to much wine, teachers of good things—that they admonish the young women to love their husbands, to love their children, to be discreet, chaste, homemakers, good, obedient to their own husbands, that the word of God may not be blasphemed.*
> —Titus 2:3–5

An older Christian woman teaches by her example and word.

GOD HAS GIVEN older women the responsibility of teaching good things to younger women. In order to be effective teachers, they must possess good character and have balanced lives. They are to teach the younger women to love their husbands and to be obedient to them, to progressively seek to understand them, and to encourage them where needed. The older woman may listen to a younger woman's marital woes, but encourage her to have an honest conversation with her husband, and to speak of him in the most respectful way possible.

She may teach the younger mothers to love their children, drawing attention to the opportunities mothers have to live godly lives before them in service, devotion, affection, and training.

She may teach women to be careful with their words and actions, and to be chaste. Discretion involves knowing when to speak and act, and when to be silent and wait. Chaste behavior is the result of keeping the mind free of impurity. Young women must be careful of what they read and watch, and those with whom they socialize.

An older woman can teach the young homemaker practical skills of scheduling, time management, cleaning, cooking, shopping, and hospitality. Young women are in need of encouragement to pursue homemaking as a worthy vocation, and to realize that nurturing their families is central to their God-given purpose.

The end result of following these instructions is that God and His Word will not be dishonored in the eyes of those outside the Christian faith.

For Your Reflection

In what areas do you need further instruction from an older woman? In what areas do you excel and could teach another woman?

The Christian Woman, Her Church and Other Activities
SERVING OTHERS

At Joppa there was a certain disciple named Tabitha, which is translated Dorcas. This woman was full of good works and charitable deeds which she did.
—Acts 9:36

A woman's role of helpmate will bear fruit in work she does for the Church.

THE WOMAN WHO wishes to know how she can serve God in the Church will learn by studying women mentioned in the New Testament. The Book of the Acts of the Apostles records the history of the women to be the first members of Christ's Church. One of the good works Dorcas did was sewing coats and garments for widows.

Mary, the mother of John Mark, opened her home for prayer meetings (Acts 12:5–17). Lydia housed visiting missionaries, like the apostle Paul (Acts 16:13–15). Phoebe gave assistance to many in times of distress or need (Rom. 16:1–2). Some served God in another way by giving their time to pray and make supplications for others (1 Tim. 5). Older women and widows, with time and discipline, can offer to pray for the Church, though every Christian woman should have a part in this important ministry.

Other good works mentioned for women are bringing up children, lodging strangers, washing the feet of saints, and relieving the afflicted (1 Tim. 5:10). A widow of the Church who has performed these tasks, and who has been married to one man, is eligible for Church support if she has no living relatives to pay for her expenses.

For Your Reflection

How will you clothe the poor, offer your home, your time and help, and your prayer for members of your church and/or other Christians?

The Christian Woman, Her Church and Other Activities
NOT RESPONSIBLE

And I do not permit a woman to teach or to have authority over a man, but to be in silence. For Adam was formed first, then Eve.
—1 Timothy 2:12–13

A woman can evaluate positions she holds in the Church.

GOD HAS CHOSEN to put men in authority of the organizations He founded, the home and the Church. Women, some of whom are Bible scholars, may be capable of teaching men, but have been asked to voluntarily concede this privilege to men out of reverence for God.

Why is it so important that women should not exercise authority over men, but rather be in submission? Man was created and given dominion over all things in the earth before Eve was created (Gen. 2). The command given to the Church by the apostle Paul has been ignored, overlooked, or reasoned away in many churches and religious organizations. Today, there are women ministers and even bishops in some churches.

A woman may have the ability and legal right to assume authority over men in arenas outside the Church, but the original Greek text of the New Testament is clear. She is to voluntarily surrender authority to the man, to whom God gave authority for His Church. She does this to express her obedience to God, who has provided the Church with instruction to maintain decency and order.

For Your Reflection

Evaluate positions you now hold in your church. Are you violating a scriptural principle by holding the position?

The Christian Woman, Her Church and Other Activities
PRIORITIES

*The fear of the L*ORD *is the beginning of wisdom, and the knowledge of the Holy One is understanding. For by me your days will be multiplied, and years of life will be added to you.*
—P<small>ROVERBS</small> 9:10–11

All of a woman's activities are not equal in importance to God.

C<small>LOSE FELLOWSHIP WITH</small> God should be a woman's first priority. She will benefit greatly from daily time set aside for prayer, reading the Bible, a devotional, singing hymns, listening, and just being still before Him. The purpose of daily devotions is to focus on God, His work, and His life. He will calm her, refresh her, and fill her with the fruit of the Holy Spirit, which is His "love, joy, peace, patience, kindness, goodness, faithfulness, gentleness, and self-control" (Gal. 5:22–23).

The person on earth to whom each wife is most responsible is her husband, and he should be her first human priority. God knows how important it is for her to be in submission to him, to honor and respect him. If he is left out of her priorities, a chain reaction of problems will occur.

If her relationship to God and her husband is sound, genuine love and concern for their children comes next. One day each Christian father and mother will stand before God and give an account of how they met their children's needs.

First Timothy 5:4–8 contains instructions about caring for those in one's house, the extended family, such as aging parents, who cannot support themselves. When a woman has met her responsibilities to God, her husband, her children, and extended family, then she is free to serve others.

F<small>OR</small> Y<small>OUR</small> R<small>EFLECTION</small>

Consider these questions before you commit to outside activities: Does this position or task violate any Scripture? How will this affect my daily time with God? What does my husband think about my taking this position? How will this affect my availability to my children? Do I have the time required to do this job with excellence?

The Christian Woman, Her Church and Other Activities
WHEN EMPLOYMENT IS REQUIRED

*She makes linen garments and sells them, and
supplies sashes for the merchants.*
—PROVERBS 31:24

An employed woman can be effective in her roles despite challenges.

IN PREVIOUS DAYS of this devotional, the topic of reflection has been the God-given role of women within marriage, home, and parenting. The tasks required of these roles are sufficient for Christian women to undertake, but when the burden of earning an income is added, the necessity of balancing priorities can cause anxiety and stress.

As a Christian woman attempts to combine a career or job outside the home with family, her greatest pressures come from herself in the form of guilt, disappointment, and frustration. She realizes that there is a limited amount of time and energy available to do her tasks in a way that meets her standards or those of others in her life.

The range of feelings for the woman who *must* earn an income differs from the woman who chooses a career or job outside the home. She may have to work because of heavy financial obligations, the desires of her husband, or because she is the sole financial provider. She may believe that God's best for her is to be a full-time mother/homemaker, but her circumstances call for something very different. Therefore her attitude toward her job may not be positive.

In order for her to enjoy her work and be effective in all her roles, she can check all her thoughts and information against Scripture and seek God regarding the situation. She may realize that she is where God wants her to be, for now. If she is married, she may discuss her feelings with her husband, who may be unaware of them. By taking an objective look at their finances, admitting the true and emotional cost of working, and seeking the steps to pay off debts, they may find a solution that would allow her to stay home. She may also discuss solutions with her present boss, as to how she could continue to work with flexible hours from home or part-time.

FOR YOUR REFLECTION

In what ways are you comparing yourself to other women instead of looking to God? If you are a single mother, have you asked your family and friends for their help?

The Christian Woman, Her Church and Other Activities
WHEN EMPLOYMENT IS NOT REQUIRED

Therefore I desire that the younger widows marry, bear children, manage the house, give no opportunity to the adversary to speak reproachfully.
—1 Timothy 5:14

A married couple can consider the true costs of the wife working outside the home.

A Christian woman's responsibilities as a wife, mother, and home manager may seem boring to her. She may experience feelings of guilt, because what "good" wife and mother does not want to care for her home and family? She may feel great stress about her home responsibilities and consider herself incapable of being a full-time homemaker because she lacks the skill, patience, and creativity required to stay home. She may fear that her brain and skills will atrophy without the stimulation of employment outside the home.

In order to make the decision whether to work or not to work outside the home, she must answer some challenging questions and seek God's will for her life. Has her husband asked her to assist him with providing income? If not, how does he feel about her sharing this role? Is he willing to help with the housework and childcare? They may become increasingly dependent on her salary so that if the wife wanted to quit working, they may not be able to afford to live as they are used to without her income. They may go into debt, running up charge accounts and loans to afford a higher lifestyle. Finally, together, they may determine before God how their family will fulfill God's purpose.

Time invested in learning the roles God has already given to a woman will take up most of her time and energy. Leisure time can be used to further her skills and interests through courses and volunteer work that may lead her to employment at a later time in her life. She will never regret having done her job well at home.

∽

For Your Reflection

How will working outside your home affect your attitude of excellence regarding your responsibilities as a wife? Mother? Home manager? How will this role affect your husband's role as provider?

CHAPTER 9

THE CHRISTIAN WOMAN, HER GROWTH AND MATURITY

The Christian Woman, Her Growth and Maturity
GROWTH AND MATURITY

For no other foundation can anyone lay than that which is laid, which is Jesus Christ.
—1 Corinthians 3:11

A woman grows and matures by depending upon God.

A WOMAN FINDS GOD'S will for her life when she reads the passages in the Bible that speak to and about women. She grows and matures as she reflects, prays, and applies these Bible truths to her everyday life. Her foundation is Jesus Christ and His principles become her convictions, to the point where living outside of them causes her to feel that she has lost her way.

The strength of her foundation is dependent on the faith she has to do what the Lord reveals to her, whether or not she feels comfortable at first. As she does this, she sees how God's wisdom and commands work, is pleased with the results, and gains confidence to put her faith into action again.

As a woman lives trustingly before God, she will encounter distraction, discouragement, and failure along the way because she is human and the adversary, Satan, does not want a Christian to live victoriously. She may not realize this possibility and try to continue by sheer determination to live obediently. No matter how determined she is, she cannot live the Christian life in her own strength. Christ overcame death and the power of sin and He will give His strength and perseverance to her, as she needs it, to make her into the woman she is supposed to be. He knows firsthand the hardships she faces and can be trusted to bring her through them.

FOR YOUR REFLECTION

Growth and maturity occur throughout the stages of your life: youth, early marriage, children at home, the empty nest, and old age. How have you seen God working in your stage of life to change you as you have reflected on these daily readings? What principles have you put into practice? How have you persevered through setbacks?

The Christian Woman, Her Growth and Maturity
GOD WILL STRENGTHEN A WOMAN'S FOUNDATION

But the Lord is faithful, who will establish you and guard you from the evil one.
—2 THESSALONIANS 3:3

Faith in Christ deepens with consistent practices.

PRAYER IS SPEAKING to God, listening to Him, and simply being still in His presence. Speaking to God consists of praise of the Lord, confession of sins, thankfulness to Him, and asking Him for help. Sometimes, no words come and just being still with Him is prayer. Listening to God is a skill acquired through consistent practice. Often a thought comes to mind during prayer that answers a question, provides direction, or brings comfort. Prayer is commanded in the Bible, and when a woman prays, she is acting in obedience to God (Matt. 6:5–15).

Daily reading and study of the Bible gives a woman a mind that establishes the Scriptures as the written testimony of Jesus Christ. This practice preserves her from private eccentricities and heresies (2 Tim. 3:14–17). No book written by man has the power of the Bible because it is a record of the actual words of God. The Holy Spirit opens her mind to understand it and does the changing work of God in her heart and life as she studies with a willing attitude.

The Holy Eucharist, (also called Holy Communion, the Lord's Supper, the Mass) is the principal act of worship set up by Christ Himself, and the means by which He strengthens His followers. He commanded that Christians gather to remember continually His life, death, and resurrection, and His coming again, by partaking in His body and blood (Matt. 28:18–20; John 6:35–58).

Consistent practice of private prayer, Bible reading, and corporate partaking of the Holy Eucharist, in obedience to Christ, will strengthen a woman's foundation and deepen her love for Him.

∽

FOR YOUR REFLECTION

How will you incorporate consistent practices to deepen your faith into your life's schedule?

POSTSCRIPT

A Christian woman who knows and practices God's design and purpose for her, no matter what age she is or in what circumstances she finds herself, can be encouraged to know that she is on God's path for her and that her life is pleasing to God.

Whenever she feels lonely and experiences persecution because of her obedience to God, she can renew her commitment by re-reading this devotional guide and asking God for fresh strength and blessing for choosing His scriptural precepts. It can be helpful to keep a journal of the many answered prayers and rewards she has experienced by following Him. These can include peace, a clear conscience, a healthy marriage, strong and godly children and grandchildren, the provision of shelter, food, good health, employment, and a church with which to worship God.

Beyond these earthly comforts, she can fix her eyes on her future destiny with God, and hope for His words to be like those of the landowner to his servant in Jesus's parable found in Matthew 25:20–21:

> So he who had received five talents came and brought five other talents, saying, "Lord, you delivered to me five talents; look, I have gained five more talents besides them." His lord said to him, "Well done, good and faithful servant; you were faithful over a few things, I will make you ruler over many things. Enter into the joy of your lord."

NOTES

MOTHERS OF CHILDREN
1. *The American Heritage Dictionary*, s.v. "character" (Boston: Houghton Mifflin Company, 1979).

HOME MANAGEMENT
1. *The American Heritage Dictionary*, s.v. "homemaker."

LOVE YOUR NEIGHBOR
1. John Piper, *Recovering Biblical Manhood and Womanhood* (Wheaton, IL: Crossway Books, 1991), 373.

OUTER BEAUTY
1. *The American Heritage Dictionary*, s.v. "attitude."

ABOUT THE AUTHOR

Holly Eggert is an author who resides with her husband in Colorado. Prior to becoming an author, she was a substitute-teaching leader, discussion leader, and children's leader with Bible Study Fellowship International and a certified instructor with TRI-R Ministries. She has served the Church as a mentor to women and led small groups with her husband that support marriages and families.

Holly is a graduate of Washington University School of Fine Arts in St. Louis and holds a BFA in graphic design. She is an accomplished graphic designer, artist, and hand quilter. She and her husband have two adult children and a daughter-in-law. They enjoy the beauty of Colorado together and spending time with family and friends.

CONTACT THE AUTHOR

You can find Holly on the Web at www.hollyeggert.com, view her profile on LinkedIn, see what she's pinning on Pinterest, and contact her personally by e-mail at holly@hollyeggert.com.